Poverty's Bonds

DATE DUE

By the same author

Killing Time, Losing Ground: Experiences of Unemployment
With a Foreword by James Rinehart

What is it like to be without a job? How does it feel to be unemployed? This book represents a much needed and refreshing departure from the usual quantitative treatments of the disadvantaged because it depicts unemployment from the perspectives of the unemployed, thus providing insights and understanding that elude statistical accounts of the phenomenon.

"An outstanding study." *(Anthony Giddens)*

"I mean, my God, we're talkin' Rejection City, here."
(One of the informants in the study)

"Burman's research developed out of his involvement with the unemployed. The outcome is a work that represents the very best of the engaged genre of sociological research."
(James Rinehart, from the Foreword)

CONTENTS
1. Setting the Stage
2. Labour Markets: The Positioning of the Unemployed
3. Labour Market Experience of the Younger and Older Unemployed
4. The Impersonal State: Manpower and Unemployment Insurance
5. The Intrusive State: Welfare and Family Benefits
6. Intermediate Organizations and Social Networks
7. The Imposed Practices of Daily Life
8. Time and the Construction of Daily Life
9. Family Relationships
10. The Self
11. Conclusions and Initiatives
Appendices / Index

ISBN 1-55077-021-7 (1988)
Thompson Educational Publishing, Inc.

Poverty's Bonds

Power and Agency in the Social Relations of Welfare

Patrick Burman
Brescia College, University of Western Ontario

THOMPSON EDUCATIONAL PUBLISHING, INC.
Toronto, Ontario

Thompson Educational Publishing, Inc.
14 Ripley Avenue, Suite 105
Toronto, Ontario M6S 3N9

Canadian Cataloguing in Publication Data

Burman, Patrick W., 1947-
        Poverty's bonds : power and agency in the social
relations of welfare

Includes bibliographical references and index.
ISBN 1-55077-077-2

1. Social service - Sociological aspects. 2. Social
service - Ontario - London. I. Title.

HM25.B87 1996   361.9713'26   C96-930092-1

Cover design: Barry Veerkamp
Printed in Canada on acid-free paper.
1 2 3 4 5   96 97 98 99 00 01 02 03 04 05

Table of Contents

Acknowledgements

I would like to acknowledge the help of Morgan Gardner, who did most of the interviewing, helped me with the analysis, and commented on early drafts. It is to her that I wish to dedicate this book.

There would have been no study without the support of the faculty members at King's College who were a part of the Social Concern group that met and explored poverty in the late 1980s, and I am appreciative.

Also I would like to thank the members of the Qualitative Methodology group (Qualms) who commented on a few early chapters. Most importantly, thanks go to the men and women who agreed to be interviewed for the study.

~~~

O my soul, I gave you all, and I have emptied all my hands
to you; and now—now you say to me smiling and full
of melancholy, "Which of us has to be thankful?
Should not the giver be thankful that the receiver received?
Is not giving a need? Is not receiving mercy?"

— *Friedrich Nietzsche,* Thus Spoke Zarathrustra

Introduction

*T*he social bonds of poverty discussed in this book are threefold, corresponding to the three senses of the word "bond" in current use. First is the bond of *covenant* which the formation of the welfare state cemented between Canada's disadvantaged and better-off citizens. Canada was to be a just society, building — out of transfers from rich to poor — a net of security and social development for all. The welfare state also tried to fill the moral vacuum created as people's ties to religion, family, and community weakened.[1] This compact between the poor and the non-poor, directed and institutionalized by successive governments, even came to be an important part of Canadian identity and pride.

The second sense of the term "bond" has a meaning both solidaristic and enabling. The notion of bond here is one of a uniting force and a community of thinking and concerned people, which one can find in the relations of low-income people with their friends, family members and other members of the community. The third meaning of bond is one of *constraint*. In archaic usage the word was a noun for slavery, and then was extended to denote anything that bound one's body in restraint of personal liberty. The figurative usage applies here: a bond is "any circumstance that trammels or takes away freedom of action" (Oxford English Dictionary). Adapted to the poor, this third sense indicates situations or relationships which impede free, self-reliant action and make one feel trapped and powerless.

This book is a study of the bonds of covenant, enablement and constraint found in the lives of low-income people, especially as they deal with service providers to get the things they need. Its

---

[1] Alan Wolfe, *Whose Keeper? Social Science and Moral Obligation*, 30.

method, plan and conceptual framework will be worked out in the
first chapter, but it may be useful to set the stage in this introduction.
We begin with an updating of the situation of poor people to the
mid-1990's, a period of rapid, drastic decline in the fortunes of the
least well-off. The last part tries to articulate a role for sociological
analysis in the face of this current crisis.

The Current Situation

Much of current poverty is the result of a dual failure — the
economy's failure to provide jobs and decent incomes for the poor,
on the one hand, and the government's decision (through the Bank
of Canada) to live with an unemployment rate between 8 and 9
percent in order to keep inflation low, on the other. Whenever the
economy heats up and employs more people, offering the possibility of raising inflation, the Bank of Canada tightens the money
supply and raises interest rates, thus slowing the economy and
reducing job creation. This is, in effect, an explicit policy strategy
of compulsory unemployment.

Not only are these macro-economic processes producing poverty
and unemployment, the subsidies to the victims of these processes
are being cut. The government is continuing the cuts to Unemployment Insurance, requiring the jobless to work longer to qualify for
payments which are smaller and shorter in duration. In 1989, when
the Mulroney government began severe UI cuts, 83 percent of
Canadians without jobs qualified for UI benefits; in 1995, less than
half (49.7 percent) of the jobless Canadians qualify. As a result,
Canada's UI system has become one of the world's worst systems,
now sixteenth out of the 19 industrial nations (leaving only Britain,
the U.S. and Japan as less generous).[2]

The covenant between the state and the poor is being broken,
or at best restructured. The federal government is downsizing and
replacing its one-time role as political orchestrator of the welfare
state with a role more akin to a blind banker. Anxious to impress
the foreign holders of Canada's debt with its progress on deficit
reduction, the federal government is off-loading its responsibilities

[2] *CCPA Monitor* (Canadian Centre for Policy Alternatives), July-August, 1995, 12.

to the provinces at a startling pace. In April 1996, the federally regulated Canada Assistance Plan (CAP) is replaced by the Canada Health and Social Transfer (CHST), which will give block grants to the provinces to cover the costs of health care, post-secondary education and welfare and social services. The provinces are now free to support the more popular social expenditures like health and education, while giving welfare and social services short shrift. Politicians' references to the "dependent" poor, who are "sitting at home collecting cheques," are designed to chime with the general public's stereotypes about the poor — thus preparing the ground for continuous cuts to the meagre resources of the disadvantaged.

With CAP's exit go the rules and conditions that the federal government used to attach to its transfers to the provinces. (The only federal rule remaining is the prohibition on restricting welfare benefits due to residency requirements — which British Columbia is currently challenging by its denial of welfare for newcomers for the first three months of their residency.) For instance, there is no longer a prohibition on making welfare recipients work for their assistance. Various forms of workfare already exist in Alberta, New Brunswick and Quebec and one is being planned for Ontario, even though studies of work-for-welfare programs in the U.S. show little benefit to those forced to work compared with those who did not participate. Of little benefit to the recipients, expensive to administer, these programs appear to function only as a tool for controlling people. The real beneficiaries seem to be the companies that take advantage of the subsidized labour. Furthermore, employability programs replace jobs, rather than create them. The Alberta Community Employment program (ACE) provides jobs to welfare recipients at $6.00 an hour. A hospital in Red Deer recently laid off many of its full-time permanent workers and replaced them with poorly-paid, inexperienced ACE workers. In Quebec, more than half of the participating companies in that province's employability program admitted that they would have hired workers at full wages if not for the province's program.[3]

Under cover of a crisis in public finances, all manner of injustice is being perpetrated in Ontario in the mid-1990s. As of late 1995

[3] Toupin, "Index on workfare," 48.

(when this is being written), the Ontario government led by Conservative premier Mike Harris has severely reduced legal aid funding, has cut its non-profit cooperative housing program, wants to abolish the drug plans for welfare recipients and seniors and intends to remove rent controls. It has closed down shelters and second-stage housing for battered women, has cut child care, has abolished employment equity, and cut back pay equity. It is planning the removal of the 100,000 permanently unemployables (those with long-term ailments such as arthritis, back pain, multiple sclerosis) from its family benefits system. And, most draconian of all, it has made 21.6 percent cuts to welfare benefits — with the avowed goal of bringing Ontario's benefit levels to a point 10 percent above the national average. In a nakedly redistributive move that contradicts its deficit reduction thrust, the Harris government has promised tax cuts of 30 percent to the middle classes. This will put approximately the same amount of dollars into well-off citizens' pockets (just under $300 a month) as the welfare cuts will take from the budgets of low-income single parents with two children!

Further down the chute of decentralization slide the poor. The municipalities, which administer welfare and pay 20 percent of its cost, are looking for ways to off-load recipients, whether onto the backs of their families, the voluntary sector, religious charities, or food banks. Many welfare officials, when they cannot provide an appointment or cheque to a desperately needy person, refer her to the local food bank. The ultimate terminus of this devolving of responsibility is, of course, the low-income person himself or herself. It is the poor mother who must provide for her family members, in spite of meagre resources and fragmentary social supports. The terrible impacts of poverty are often suffered in isolation. The result is a kind of implosion, a bursting-within, in the psyches and relationships of the poor that is barely perceptible in the surface calm of mainstream society.

In contrast to this isolating impact of poverty, however, are signs of proactive, even explosive, community and political mobilization. London, Ontario, was chosen by union officials as the focus of a one-day strike and day of protest against the brutal cuts to social programs made by the Harris government. On December 11, 1995, an estimated ten thousand unionists, poor people, community activists and other citizens converged on and marched in London. On a daily basis, community groups are finding ways to help poor people get food, to oppose or cope with evictions, and to develop strategies with the poor and public officials to deal with the large numbers of people in desperate straits.

The Role for an Engaged Sociological Analysis

Ascendant neo-conservative governments and ideologies use low-income people on benefits as a scapegoat for a politics of resentment. They are, in effect, urging non-poor citizens to raise the threshold of their response to the pain of the disadvantaged. Slogans about the passive or fraudulent nature of "those people on welfare" are the anesthetic which dulls our capacity to feel and know the sufferings of the poor.

I believe that sociological research and analysis of the situation of low-income people may legitimately — without sacrificing methodological or conceptual standards — take the standpoint of those thrust below the threshold of societal awareness and empathy. Sociology should be a science concerned with situations and groups below the threshold of public visibility.[4] Doing in-depth research with marginal groups not only uncovers suppressed perspectives on life conditions, it gives us a unique and necessary vantage point on contemporary modes of domination. The questions raised by an engaged sociology would be of the following type: "Who, by virtue of the way we live and think, are not being heard, not being accorded freedom, not acting as subject, not formulating their own demands or needs, and especially not having public attention given to the dire and unfair costs levied on them by the policies and freedoms of the powerful?"

A critical sociology ought to be prepared to debunk all human constructions which are passed off by their (elite) partisans as law-like and necessary — the "things we have to accept and adjust to" — particularly when it is the poor that is doing the adjusting. At issue here are the conditioning frameworks of discourse and

---

[4] Wolfe, *Whose Keeper?*, 209. He draws from Victor Turner, *The Ritual Process: Structure and Anti-structure*. Chicago: Aldine, 1969.

action whereby the elites try to define the limits of the possible in ways that serve their own interests. Critical sociology ought to analyze "power language," whose abstractions mask the humanly constructed domination currently in play and screen out the realities of people's lives and their opportunities for resistance. After all, we live in a day when graphs and tables often appear to provide the abstract justification for inflicting societal pain. Examples would be the federal government's determination to hold the unemployment rate at the non-inflating levels of between 8 and 9 percent and the Harris government's cutting the Ontario welfare rates to a level no more than 10 percent above the Canadian average.

Social science should be one of the resources of a humane society. Whether or not sociologists become involved in their community or in politics is an individual choice, but actively engaging in the community is not only good in itself but ultimately enriches our knowledge. This study, which is aimed mostly at understanding the situations in which the poor find themselves, is offered in solidarity with them and all those who work in their interests. Perhaps the intention of the book is best expressed by the British cultural critic Stuart Hall: "The work that cultural studies has to do is to mobilize everything that it can find in terms of intellectual resources in order to understand what keeps making the lives we live, and the societies we live in, profoundly and deeply anti-humane."[5] I subscribe to this view wholeheartedly.

---

[5] Quoted in hooks, *Outlaw Culture*, 3.

1

Conceptual, Historical and Ideological Context

*T*his is a sociological study of the relationships between givers and receivers in the welfare state. The heart of the book is based on interviews with low-income people and service providers conducted in London, Ontario, in 1989. There are chapters on coping, receiving, and acting, which are based on the reported experiences of low-income informants, and chapters on the modes of giving based on accounts by service providers. But, in this first chapter, we need to establish the context — historical, conceptual and ideological — of contemporary relations between givers and receivers. The attention given to history will, I think, be justified as the reader learns of the extensive continuities between past and present attitudes towards the poor and modes of giving.

Poverty is relational, and an integral part of the workings of mainstream society. It is not fundamentally about attributes of persons facing economic hardship, but about the wrenching and realignment of personal projects, relationships and exchanges following on hardship. In commodified market space, the low-income person experiences an alien feeling amid discrete exclusions. She may not feel fully visible, or feel that she belongs — except as service employee or window-shopper. In the job market, the low-income individual may come to regard good jobs as parts for which she will never get an audition, lacking as she does the desired dress and look, the lines, the contacts. In *social* space, she will draw strength from her close relationships, but will discover that she is no longer viewed by the public as a person worthy of respect, but rather as a member of a disreputable social category. When forced to turn to providers of services and food, for instance, she will find herself treated and regarded in a variety of unusual roles: as client, as lost sheep, as socialization project, as potential activist, as bearer of innumerable deficits that providers are disposed to fill. The low-income person may find herself cast as a figure in a moral allegory that is as old as the Bible and as deeply sedimented as the culture's most basic moral values.

This relational field of social space involves, at a minimum, an intersubjective co-production of meaning by both provider and client. Hewitt, citing C. Offe, suggests a potential sharing of purpose in the fundamental relation of this field:

> The "product" the client receives from the service agency involves an act of collaboration: the producer identifies the individual needs of the client; and the client co-operates in interactive work with the provider, and only thereby completes the product.... [6]

Others have given to the concept of field a more competitive sense, as in Bourdieu's notion of "field of power":

> By field of power, I mean the relations of force that obtain between the social positions which guarantee their occupants a quantum of social force, or of capital, such that they are able to enter into the struggles over the monopoly of power, of which struggles over the definition of the legitimate form of power are a crucial dimension. [7]

In another strong and generalized sense, the field of relations may have the service provider helping to "constitute" the client who is led to conform to the provider's mode of helping, and thus helps constitute and empower the provider. Whatever the adequacy of these models to the varieties of modes of helping brought out in the research, it is this mutually conditioned social space between poor and provider that is the principal terrain explored in this book. More precisely, the inquiry — drawing from interviews with service providers and low-income individuals — focuses on the interplay between service providers' configurations of roles and subject-positions of their "clients" (along with the providers' linked self-presentations) *and* the responses of low-income people who either enact those subject-positions, distance themselves from, or resist them.

The study is more meaning-oriented than structural, bringing out the discursive or ideological dimension of the relations and practices of welfare.[8] Like Nancy Fraser, I do not consider this dimension

---

[6] Hewitt, *Welfare, Ideology and Need*, 127.

[7] Bourdieu, *Invitation to a Reflexive Sociology*, 229-230.

[8] "Welfare" (upper case) refers to government benefits, while "welfare" (lower case) takes in the whole gamut of helping and beneficial practices.

as distinct from welfare practices, but rather comprising "the tacit norms and implicit assumptions that are constitutive of those practices."[9] Uncovering those may help us make sense of diverse programs and modes of helping, but, even more revealingly (in this case keyed to gender),

> could illuminate what I called "the politics of need interpretation," since it could expose the processes by which welfare practices construct women and women's needs according to certain specific — and in principle contestable — interpretations.[10]

Now these constructions (of identities, needs, subject-positions, etc.) are interpreted identities and needs and often quite political; part of their power as ideologically guided interpretations lies precisely in the concealment of their interpreted character and the lack of influential counter-interpretations. It is imperative that these interpretations be subjected to analysis and critique — playing them off in part against known patterns of social inequality, but also against the freely expressed identities and needs of low-income persons themselves.

As mentioned, this chapter looks briefly at the conceptualization and measurement of poverty and need, the historical background of relations between poor and non-poor, some ideological currents in the welfare state, and the restructuring of the political economy affecting the poor. Then follows a description of the research.

Defining and Measuring Poverty and Need

The different definitions of poverty and need can be placed, roughly, on a scale from minimalist to more inclusive. For poverty there are monetized and non-monetized definitions; for need there are "thin" and "thick" conceptions. These basic variants need to be sketched at the outset, along with the approach of this study.

In the monetized definition of poverty, the main concern is where to place the income line which distinguishes the poor from the

---

[9] See Fraser, "Women, Welfare," 146.

[10] Ibid.

non-poor and how to measure it (i.e., what should be included as income and what is the most valid income data source). In the calculation of the Statistics Canada Low-Income Cut-Offs (LICO), the government agency analyzes family expenditure data to determine what percentage of the average family's income is spent on food, shelter and clothing (54.7 percent in the 1992 survey). That figure is then marked up, arbitrarily, by 20 percentage points, and the resulting figure (74.7 percent in 1992, adjusted in years when there is no consumer survey according to changes in the consumer price index) is the low-income cut-off. Families who spend more than the cut-off percentage for basic essentials are seen as low income. In the figuring of the LICOs, family size and community size are accommodated, yielding 35 separate cut-offs.[11] So in 1992, Statistics Canada chose a sample of 39,000 households to acquire its data, covering all Canadian households except for residents of the northern territories, Aboriginal Canadians on reserves, and the inmates of institutions. The survey's measure of income took in wages and salaries (pre-deductions), net income from self-employment, government transfer payments, investment income, pension and alimony income and the like.

The fact that the LICOs are pegged to changing patterns of average Canadian families introduces a widely accepted *relative* element in the poverty measure (as opposed to a purely "absolute" measure). Other measures go farther towards a purely relative approach. The Canadian Council of Social Development considers the poverty line to be one-half of average income — thus being more a measure of inequality than poverty. Other approaches, like that of the Metropolitan Toronto Social Planning Council, combine an objective, shopping-basket method with a built-in relative aspect. The Council "seeks to identify a selection of goods and services whose cost represents the minimum expenditure necessary for social — rather than merely physical — survival."[12] The limitation here is the weak generalizability of the measure beyond Toronto.

---

[11] See Ross, Shillington, and Lochhead, *Canadian Fact Book*, 13.

[12] Ibid., 18.

Non-monetary definitions, though less precise and useful for quantitative comparisons, go beyond income poverty to the protean empirical aspects of being poor. Here poverty is seen as falling behind the standards and dimensions of well-being of society, as experiencing a relative deprivation. Townsend, very pertinently for this study, sees as a marker of poverty "the inability to participate in the usual social exchanges of society."[13] To be without a telephone, for example, is to be relatively deprived in Canada, even if not in, say, rural Zimbabwe. With urban civilization increasing the need for infrastructural, educational and technical supports, the search for a more comprehensive definition of poverty leads us directly to examples or indices of the non-monetary (dys)functioning of low-income life. A modern instance of this would be Sweden's social accounting system which monitors people's relative progress on nine dimensions of well-being: employment and working conditions, educational access and knowledge, health, housing, security of life and property, leisure activities, and political resources. Information is gathered about groups which fall behind, with a special attention given to gender, class, age and regional differences.[14]

A further example may make the point. In an analysis deriving from Max Weber's concept of "status," Miller underscores a crucial deficit of poverty: group self-respect.[15] The poor suffer from low group self-respect, deriving from internalized stigma. If low-income children are deprived of a rich, high-expectancy education, they grow up thinking themselves "irretrievably limited in the kind of work they can perform."[16] (Example: many Latinos in the United States agree with the dominant view that they do not speak good English.) Later, if group members are barred from careful work through discrimination, they may see themselves as incapable of doing this kind of work. "The oppressed thus limit themselves. Accepting the others' view of one's group can be very damaging."[17]

---

[13] Cited in Miller, "Poverty and respect," 4.

[14] Mullally, "Social welfare," 79.

[15] Miller, "Poverty and respect," 21.

[16] Ibid., 24.

[17] Ibid.

So to be without this critical dimension of well-being — group self-respect — is to risk being plunged into a well of widening disadvantage. Only by such analyses as these, perhaps, will we arrive at inductive, empirically fleshed-out characterizations of poverty as it is experienced.

In the orientations towards *need* as well, a similar trajectory extends from minimalist to more expansive. "Thin" conceptions of need tend to be objectivist and ostensibly universal, e.g., the need for food and shelter. These and other material and social minima can be formulated and counted by experts, and can be defended as being within government's purview to monitor and underwrite. Now, when the formulation of needs that are addressable through state provision "thickens" — i.e., becomes more discursively elaborated by non-experts, especially affected persons and groups — thin advocates tend to object. Economists argue that the notion of demand is more reliable in allocating scarce resources among competing ends. The concern is that indiscriminate need-formation by groups is a "Pandora's box." Della Nevitt uses the term "needology":

> purporting to discover new requirements on the part of any and every disadvantaged group, without adequate criteria for comparing different groups or justifying the allocation of resources to those particular ends.[18]

We should engage in the comparative study, such thinkers argue, of the effects of social policy — breaking out of the prescriptivist assumptions of those committed to the improvement of their single society.

So what is the justification offered by the proponents of the "thick" conception of needs? More than the scientific validation of the claims to real needs, there must be "normative validation of their democratic acceptability to citizens of a welfare state."[19] When

---

[18] Cited in Bulmer, Lewis, and Piachaud, *Goals of Social Policy*, 14.

[19] Hewitt's quote (*Welfare, Ideology and Need*, 178) suggests Habermas, who is important to his and my work in this study. Habermas's approach privileges a realm of communicative rationality wherein there would be discursive redemption of claims to needs. There may be scientific validation of the substance of need-claims, but this would not be an autonomous process shaped by scientists and managers, but a process co-determined by research specialists and people grounded in the communicative rationality of their lifeworld. Habermas called this the dialectic of potential and will.

needs claims thicken, they become less general and more embedded in people's projects as they confront authority figures and
gatekeepers; they enter the contested sphere of politics. We need
X, but always to pursue some further purpose ("in order to attain
or achieve Y"). We do not measure the harm done by the unmet
need according to an objective standard; rather we assert the moral
weight of our sequence of claims which is meant to oblige the
onlooker to answer it.[20] Take the example of Fraser's unravelling
of the particular forms of provision needed by homeless people
beyond the thin need of being sheltered from the elements: "Do
homeless people need forbearance so that they may sleep undis-
turbed next to a hot-air vent on a street corner? A space in a subway
tunnel or a bus terminal? ... A permanent home? Suppose we say
the latter. What kind of permanent housing do homeless people
need?."[21] Depending on what *background assumptions* people
make, the unravelling of these chains of in-order-to relations lead
to very different termini: to a questioning, say, of the priorities and
exclusions of commercial real estate in the city, or, oppositely, to
an insistence that people be rousted out of their outdoor refuges
and placed in detention.

The position of this study, in short, leans towards an inclusive,
multiform conception of poverty and a thick, inductive presentation
of needs. These choices do the most justice to the record of the
lived experience of the interviewees in the study. These choices,
as well, afford the best purchase on the reciprocal and contested
relationships between needs claimants and service providers. The
normative standpoint of the study is that of the disadvantaged.

Historical Background: Relations between Poor and Non-Poor

In the feudal period social security was organized in a land tenure
system which delegated property by a lord to a serf. The serf
worked the land for the lord and received in return home, food,
community and forms of care in sickness and old age. This secure

---

[20] Kerans, "Need and welfare," 54.

[21] Fraser, "Women, Welfare," 163.

(though sometimes tyrannical) bond came at a cost for the serfs: they had no freedom to leave their villages without permission and to pursue labour elsewhere. Apart from the land system, vagrants and other alms-seekers went to the monasteries and churches for charity. Underlying these charitable acts of medieval poor relief was an ethic which upheld the dignity and rights of the needy.

With the break-up of feudalism (and the closing of monasteries in England), the older ethic lost its societal influence. The poor were increasingly being seen as "untrustworthy, dangerous, immoral and inferior."[22] Their poverty and unemployment was regarded as self-chosen and motivated by the desire to avoid work. At first, poor relief measures were instituted to cope with the destitute, who had become unwelcome elements in a fragmenting, individualizing economic scene. A relief fund made up of voluntary contributions was set up in the local jurisdictions, but harsh punishments were meted out to discourage vagrancy and begging.[23] This "support" was amplified into public policy in England by the Elizabethan poor law legislation of 1601 — which was the first step on the road to the welfare state. Tax revenues were made available to local parishes to establish almshouses for the sick and elderly, work-houses for the able-bodied poor, correctional houses or even jail for those who would not agree to work, and some apprentice training for poor people's children. Whatever the intent of the laws, the reality was very harsh. To cut costs, parish authorities crowded the vagrants, mentally ill, children and sick into miserable poor-houses — which had the strong, indirect effect of stiffening the discipline of the workers who were employed:

> The individual clung to his or her job when the only alternative to work, no matter how onerous or ill-paid, was a choice between starvation or the parish workhouse with its penal atmosphere, the risk of contagion from infectious diseases, and the ignominy of being labelled a "pauper."[24]

It may be inferred from this that the power of market space — in this case, of employers to keep their workers" "feet to the fire" with

---

[22] Heidenheim, "Political Economy", 48.

[23] Guest, *Emergence of Social Security*, 9.

[24] Ibid., 11.

poor working conditions and low pay — was enhanced by the visibly degrading character of the workhouse. With market space as the point of reference for social space, the benefits of the latter were always kept less eligible than those of the former.

The poor laws were instituted in Nova Scotia and New Brunswick in the mid-eighteenth century. Townships and counties were obliged to collect funds for the relief of the destitute and needy, and to provide for asylums and other institutions as needed. Lacking the density of population and tax base of England, however, and possessing a highly mobile immigrant population, the eastern colonies introduced aberrant forms of the poor law system. Poor rural parishes started the practice of contracting out the care of their indigent to the lowest bidder, and even held annual public auctions of paupers, in some areas. Inquests after the deaths of paupers under the "care" of this system showed evidence of intentional neglect and physical abuse. A public workhouse in Nova Scotia for both adults and children, according to Turner, "for many years dealt out whippings, shacklings, starvation, and other such inducements to correct the behaviour of reluctant or vagrant inmates."[25]

In Quebec, or Lower Canada, welfare institutions for farmers, workers and the needy were run by the Catholic Church and its orders (with the help of lay managers), which were given a state charter but no regular grants. In Ontario, or Upper Canada, legislation passed in 1792 adopted English civil law while intentionally excluding a poor law. This was done partly to avoid strengthening the quasi-republican powers of local jurisdictions, partly because so many opportunities were thought to be available so as to make public relief unnecessary. The effect of the exclusion was that the government shifted responsibility for the poor to the individual, the family, and the private philanthropist. Government's "policy," then, was initially negative — often using punitive measures to bolster the determination of the individual to look out for his/her own welfare. Government aimed to "protect society from undesirables, such as criminals, delinquents, the poor, and the mentally ill."[26] In early Upper Canada history the "the jails became

---

[25] Turner, "The Historical Base," 51-52.

[26] Ibid., 52.

a type of poorhouse — a catch-all for a variety of social problems —
the homeless poor, the insane, the offenders, both petty and serious,
young and old."[27] The government reluctantly increased its welfare
role: building penitentiaries and hospitals, underwriting (but not
obliging) the formation of municipal welfare institutions, providing
a patchwork of grants to charities who helped out the destitute
immigrant and the jobless.

Industrialization in the Post-Confederation Period

Up to the early 1940s, the Canadian government was a reluctant
provider of welfare, backing into its eventual leading role with
limited, reactive steps. This was true even in the years when Canada
industrialized in the late 1800s, a process which gave poverty its
modern shape. Industrialization broke down the patterns of independent work on the farm and in the shops of trades and craft
workers, and replaced them with wage labour in manufacturing
establishments. Propertyless workers from rural areas competed
with the newly arrived immigrants for jobs in the rapidly expanding
Canadian cities. In these emerging labour markets, employers
sought an unskilled, flexible workforce, so that they could keep
wage costs low and profits high, and could hire or lay off workers
according to the boom or bust phase of the economy. In the slums
and shantytowns of the cities in the late 1800s, many people were
steeped in Third World conditions. Living in crowded, cold-water
flats, families barely subsisted on the wages the husband earned
working sixty hours a week, fifty-two weeks a year. Winters often
brought layoffs and meagre earnings would now be brought in by
the wife and children. Families suffered all manner of torments:
illness, poor heating and sanitation, accidents, disability, high infant
mortality, recession. Montreal, for example,

> was the most dangerous city in the western world to be born in.
> Between 1899 and 1901, 26.76 percent of all new born children
> died before they were one year old. This was more than double
> the figure for New York and was ... lower than only one larger
> city — Calcutta. These statistics were largely the result of unsafe
> water, impure milk and the limited use of vaccination against
> smallpox and diphtheria.[28]

---

[27] Guest, *Emergence of Social Security*, 13.

[28] Copp, 1974:193-194.

In the poor sections of the city where these death and disease rates were highest, desperate parents turned their children over to orphanages, or they were "apprenticed out as servants, placed as factory workers, or left to the streets."[29]

Along with the individualism underwritten (by default) by a reluctant state, there sprang up private philanthropists and a spate of non-governmental groups. Voluntary, charitable, often religious organizations ministered to the needs of immigrants and the disadvantaged. Organizations which targeted political, economic and moral reform began to stir. Citizen groups in communities gathered basic necessities in the harsh winters to give to the "worthy poor," thus keeping them off humiliating public relief. There were women's temperance groups, associations for social reform of prisons and subsidies for the poor, socially conscious church groups (following the "social gospel"), and a host of others promoting housing, health, recreation for children and education for women. Rising unions were making demands for better working conditions and a family wage. There were radical workers' organizations, often immigrant-led, as well as farmers' and producers' co-operatives. But, from the vantage point of the poor who had dealings with these groups, there were negative and positive aspects. Fragmentary, *ad hoc* in character, often driven by crisis (e.g., winter hardship, economic recession, typhoid epidemics), these groups did not achieve comprehensive solutions to the problems of poverty and inequality. The more established among them came to require government grants and found themselves more monitored and bureaucratized than before. In turn, they often preached to, controlled, and patronized their low-income clients. In a more positive vein, many of their number were public-spirited and wanted to include all in one human family. They were the first citizen-participants in the community and public grappling with the serious social problems of their time.

Gradually, state involvements in meeting people's social and economic needs increased. Beyond its occasional aid to institutions for capital costs and maintenance, Ontario institutionalized grants-in-aid with the Charity Aid Act of 1874, benefiting institutions for

---

[29] Duffy and Mandell, "The widening gap," 54.

the deaf, the blind and the mentally retarded. After Confederation, inspections of institutions increased, school attendance became regulated, public health rules and procedures were set, and there was monitoring of work conditions in the factories. The appearance of destitute urban waifs on the streets prompted child protection legislation and the founding of the Children Aid Society. All in all, despite these (largely reactive) legislative, regulative and funding developments as well as the various inquiries into social welfare (prompted often by women's and other reform groups), "no major state social expenditure programmes were instituted or pro- posed."[30]

The Ideological Project against Pauperism

Before looking at the ideologies and structuring of the present- day welfare state, we need to extract from the past relations of poor and non-poor some conceptual guideposts that may orientate us in the present. How did the ideologies of some of the historical providers to low-income people configure the recipients of their services?

Individualism and self-reliance were prized by the settlers, who were excited by the opportunities of free enterprise in the new world. Poverty was the unavoidable lot of many even able-bodied settlers and public sympathy (and haphazard relief) was extended. But what was truly despised was dependence on others, which was felt to be shameful and stigmatizing. Individualistic explanations of poverty came naturally to a frontier society and to be a pauper was to be seen as one who had a character flaw or failing. Guest extends Weber's "Protestant ethic" thesis to this domain:

> [S]uccess [was interpreted] as evidence of godly living and of God's grace. The corollary was, of course, that poverty was an indication of a sinful life and of divine retribution. Therefore such help as was extended to the poor was often accompanied by unsolicited and largely irrelevant advice on how the poor might regain God's grace through the exercise of those human qualities which He apparently admired and rewarded. The poor were urged to appreciate the values of thrift, hard work, self-help, and

---

[30] Moscovitch and Drover, "Social expenditures," 20.

self-discipline. Biblical tracts pointing the way to spiritual salvation were popular items for distribution to the poor. A particular danger for the poverty-stricken, according to the conventional wisdom, was addiction to strong drink, which in a government report of 1849 was blamed for one-half to two-thirds of the insanity, and three-fourths of the paupers in the Province of Canada.[31]

The pauper was seen, then, as a morally flawed individual whose plight became a project of redemptive activity by the helpers. But this was only one of the subject-positions assigned to the poor in the social space growing alongside market space in early capitalism. This was one of the older "channels" in a newly modulated flow of power in liberal capitalism. We will look more carefully into social space.

Social space in early capitalism became a domain for the exercise of techniques of power appropriate to a society of ostensibly free citizens being moulded into the contours of an ostensibly free market economy. The dominant configuring groups in social space were social economists, philanthropists, administrators, doctors and others. Their ultimate project — notwithstanding their personal motives and stated aims — was to graft morality onto economics, i.e., to introduce technologies to achieve change in people's behaviour with a view toward reconciling them to the economic project of wealth creation.[32] Their techniques and discourses were no less important to emerging capitalism than that of the industrialists and economists in market space. Out of strife, their project was to create order, which was seen not as the opposite of freedom, but its *condition*. It was to create social happiness, which is "part of an articulated project which brings into relation distinct sectors of the population and takes control of their reciprocal connections.[33] More specifically, they were shaping recalcitrant elements to follow the new imperatives created by the free infusion of capital into the cycle of production, distribution, exchange and consumption. These imperatives were that people be subjectified as self-monitoring and motivated workers and consumers.

---

[31] Guest, *Emergence of Social Security*, 16.

[32] Procacci, "Social economy," 158.

[33] Ibid., 156.

The raw material they worked on was whatever persons or groups would not fit into (and submit to) these imperatives. What was worked on was not merely the poor — because, though bereft of means, their yearnings and directions may already be on the path towards self-interested market space — but *pauperism*. The pauperized urban masses were feared as an anti-society, a drifting inchoate aggregate of the uninitiated — ripe, perhaps, for recruitment into an oppositionist proletarian class. Gordon refers to the danger "to an anxious bourgeoisie ... represented by the indiscipline, the asocial autonomy" of the paupers.[34] The social economists had, as their socialization project, the suppression of such "amoral, pre-industrial solidarities ... [so that] the free circulation of labour and capital which is the *sine qua non* of liberal welfare" will be unblocked.[35]

Procacci describes pauperism in a way that shows both its perceived dangers and the answering stratagems of the social economists:

> Pauperism is thus poverty intensified to the level of *social danger*: the spectre of the mob; a collective, essentially urban phenomena ... It is a magma in which are fused all the dangers which beset the social order, shifting along unpredictable, untraceable channels of transmission and aggregation. It is insubordinate, hidden from the scrutinizing gaze of any governing instance.[36]

All natural, uncivilized inclinations (e.g., drinking, carousing, fornicating, spending unwisely, etc.) are to be converted into channels that are satisfied by and supportive of the orderly project of wealth creation in the liberal regime. The real referent of the term "pauperism" is not concrete poor people in their lived reality, but "the ensemble of adversities/adversaries which confront the project of social order."[37] The enemy of the social economists' project — against which are deployed the techniques of combat, of restraint, guidance, or societal engineering — is the difference and discontinuity of pauperism. As for poverty itself, it is expected to remain.

---

[34] Gordon, "Governmental Rationality," 31.

[35] Ibid., 37-38.

[36] Procacci, "Social economy," 158-159.

[37] Ibid., 163, emphasis added.

"Inequality is never taken as being a target for attack, but as a 'natural,' irrefutably given fact of industrial society."[38]

This project of order is well illustrated by a study of the "rescue" of charity children from "disreputable family settings and the freedom of the streets"[39] in the Atlantic provinces in the nineteenth century. When low-income parents had fallen onto hard times — for reasons such as unemployment, low wages, illness, marital desertion, alcoholism — they signed their younger children over (for a regular fee) to the total custody of orphan asylums managed by women. More humanely organized than houses of industry, poor houses, or prisons, these institutions still isolated the children from the parents who could not care for them, and from the neighbourhoods they grew up in. The Ladies Committee came to believe

> that their institutions were superior to uncontrolled working-class family life. To permit indiscriminate association at school and in play was to throw away all their hard-won advantages. Not only were the homes selective in whom they admitted but the attempts at creating a well ordered asylum within a disordered world offered a special moral environment for the proper rescue of the children selected.[40]

Economic distress drove the older children of the poor onto the streets to eke out a living. There they begged, stole, seduced, or played tambourine in the public houses; afterwards they found shelter from the elements in outhouses, sewers and dog kennels. The reaction of the social philanthropists is conveyed by this excerpt from the first annual report of the Halifax Industrial and Ragged School:

> In all large cities there is a number of boys and girls growing up under influences that mould and shape them for evil and not for good ... These are the heathen at our own doors, and worse then heathen; Arabs in the city; the standing reproach to our Christianity. These form the dangerous class in every community.[41]

As part of their reclamation into "the paths of industry and virtue"[42] (a revealing phrase of the time), the boys' freedom was taken away,

---

[38] Ibid., 158.

[39] Rooke and Schnell, "Guttersnipes and charity," 91.

[40] Ibid., 98.

[41] Cited in ibid., 91.

[42] Cited in ibid.

as they were pressed into paper making, nail manufacturing, chimney sweeping, or were indentured into farm labour with other families. Many were arrested for theft and vagrancy, which put them into provincial prison for three to six months where they made brooms, brushes, and bricks and hammered granite. Girls in prison would cook, wash and mend clothes; out of prison, they would often be indentured into private homes for domestic labour, and their education would be neglected. In short, the community responses to this moral and class dissonance within its midst, though sometimes well-intentioned, took the form of a moralized discipline and a moralized economic exploitation.

As this study will show, the colonization of this terrain of the social *remains* a project of some of the poor's service providers to this day. But once again we return to the historical background of poverty, focusing on the early years of the welfare state.

The Emerging Welfare State in the Post-war Years

The Great Depression of the 1930s, with its extensive and persistent unemployment, finally broke down the federal government's reluctance to assume national social security responsibilities. Private charities and religious organizations were simply inadequate provisioners for the multitude of jobless, and the federal government's *ad hoc* supports to municipal and provincial governments failed to meet their crippling relief burdens. A strong field of reformist and oppositionist groups — including unions, churches, women's and other social justice organizations, social workers, the jobless, social policy academics and civil servants, and the leftist party, the Co-operative Commonwealth Federation (C.C.F.) — pressured the government to respond to the unmet needs of the jobless with federal initiatives. A more inclusive, extended safety net would be required to provide for the casualties of the market system and (in the intention of the elites) to avoid unrest, and it would have to be tied together with continuing federal revenues and legislation. According to the newly influential doctrines of John Maynard Keynes, it was thought that only the federal government had the tax base and control over money supply to correct for economic downturns. It would engage in deficit spending to bolster the incomes (and spending power) of the unemployed in recessionary times and would build up a surplus out of tax revenues in more promising economic times.

A critical fork in the road of the emerging Canadian welfare state appeared between 1940 and 1945, pointing in one direction to social democracy and in another, to liberal residualism. The Rowell-Sirois Report of 1940 dealt with federal-provincial responsibilities and jurisdictions in the important areas of unemployment insurance, old age pensions, social security, minimum wage, hours of work and regional disparities. But far more influential was the Beveridge Report from Britain, which came out in 1942 and had the effect of galvanizing many Canadian reformers. Sir William Beveridge's report established full employment as a nationally planned goal, which was not to be left to the private market. It championed comprehensive social insurance to protect the employment incomes of all, comprehensive health insurance to protect people's health, and children's allowances going to parents regardless of income. It spoke of providing for housing, education of children, disability, and old age. Three advantages were cited by Beveridge for this plan:

> It called for contributions from all who were gainfully employed and thus could not be said to provide something for nothing; it was universal in its application thereby expunging any notion of charity and it was a first step toward giving those who were fighting a positive aim and not merely a negative one of avoiding defeat.[43]

In the same spirit three major Canadian governmental studies were published that argued for comprehensive social security, housing and urban planning, and health insurance.[44] The Marsh Report on social security called for full employment, buttressed by government job creation, especially in public works. It argued for comprehensive, federally financed and administered social insurance protection and, when the benefits were exhausted, national social assistance payments (as well as family allowances). The Marsh and Heagerty Reports advocated comprehensive, universal, and contributory health insurance.

---

[43] Guest, "World War II," 206.

[44] Canada, *Report on Social Security* (Marsh report); Canada, *Housing and Community* (Curtis report); and Canada, *Health Insurance* (Heagerty report).

But the opposition to this push for comprehensive social welfare legislation was powerful and strategically placed in Mackenzie King's cabinet. Led by C.D. Howe, the Minister of Munitions and Supply, an elite group of civil servants and politicians convinced the prime minister that piecemeal social reforms would be sufficient to placate the returning troops and to blunt the appeal of the left-wing C.C.F. party. What was needed was government's removal of the scaffolding of national planning and its avid support for industry's conversion to peace-time capitalism, wherein a thriving free market would provide for people's needs and demands.[45] Capitalism *did* boom again in the post-war period and many Canadians gratefully accepted its rewards and opportunities.

Supported by tax revenues of businesses and employed Canadians as well as comparatively low inflation, the Canadian state — at least up until the mid-seventies — expanded the scope of its welfare legislation and social programs. With an adequate material base, the federal government was able to respond positively to the demands of groups in the 1960s and 70s (such as women, minorities, the young, the elderly, etc.) for support in their efforts to join the mainstream of Canadian society. The Unemployment Insurance Act was made over in 1971 to include virtually all employed Canadians and to provide disability, maternity and fishers' benefits. A Guaranteed Income Supplement was added to Old Age Security, public housing programs were initiated (and eventually non-profit co-operative housing), medicare was established, along with many other programs such as employment equity and pay equity.

But the vision and practice of a collectively ordered welfare society — with its promise of freedom from want and comprehensive entitlements to employment, health and social security — had not been supported by the elites in that critically formative time in the early 1940s. They had opted for a residualist, liberal-capitalist model, which would have to be accommodated to the fundamental business directions in the economy. So with the rapid inflation of the 1970s came the demise of the Keynesian emphasis on redistributing to the demand side. The focus shifted to supply-side strategies

---

[45] See Guest, "World War II," and Moscovitch and Drover, "Social expenditures," for more analysis of this critical time.

to control inflation whatever its consequences for the unemployment rate. Indeed the welfare state is being restructured so as to be less supportive to the disadvantaged, while food banks and other non-state supports are increasingly being relied on.

The Welfare State: Ideological Conflict and Structural Change

There is a fundamental duality underlying liberal civil society which structures not only group oppositions but mental categories such as typologies and ideological frameworks. The duality took its clearest and most dramatic shape in nineteenth-century France.[46] Property confers citizenship, in that one has a body and labour power to sell, but the expression of that citizenship is mediated by the power of the employer who owns the means of production. From this flows two incompatible ideas of economic citizenship:

> citizenship as the right to work, or the obligation of the state to ensure for its citizens the minimum conditions of their economic existence and citizenship as the right to property, affirmed against the feared violation of economic citizenship by confiscatory nationalizations.[47]

In the contested zone between these two poles have occurred many of the clashes of French, and our own, history. The French constitutions after 1815 gave enormous power to the industrial capitalist, while keeping the labouring masses wholly subordinate in rights and benefits. The revolutions of 1848 and the Commune of 1871 were organized attempts by the excluded population to form a civil society that guaranteed *its* right to economic and social citizenship. The formative results of this primal conflict were, for our purposes, twofold. Firstly, the *state* takes on new roles — regulative, disciplinary, tutelary, redistributive — which interpenetrate with civil society. Variously interventionist and disengaged, the state finds its agenda and non-agenda[48] a key point of contention by the combatants of civil society. Secondly, the established powers of capitalist society, anxious to avoid revolutionary ferment among

---

[46] Gordon's "Governmental Rationality" is an important conceptualizer of this history.

[47] Ibid., 28.

[48] Ibid., 29.

the disaffected masses, attempt to reconstruct the poor as disciplined adherents of its own model of economic citizenship. This
social incorporation of the underclass into capitalist society becomes a societal project of vast size.

Two instructive typologies of welfare states, which are implicitly
structured by the aforementioned duality, enable us to contextualize
the *Canadian* welfare state. According to Esping-Andersen,[49] there
are three regime-clusters of welfare states: conservative-corporatist,
social democratic, and liberal. The "conservative-corporatist" group,
which includes Austria, France, Italy, and Germany, uses state
welfare measures to bolster traditional status differentials based on
family and church affiliation. Society-wide redistribution is minimal,
benefits are qualified by the family's ability to pay, and there is little
in the way of day care and protection of working women's wages
to upset the traditional gendered order of families. The "social-
democratic" regime-type includes a small number of states like
Sweden and Norway and, to a lesser extent, Denmark and Finland.
Many of the programs are de-commodifying and universalistic,
aimed at offering a high welfare standard to all based on social
right. Though taxes are high, full employment policies ensure a
modest proportion of people living off social transfers. Family
prerogatives give way to children's rights, and individual women's
rights to work and train and attain social mobility. (In Titmuss's
well-known conceptualization, this would be the "institutional"
welfare type.[50])

It is the "liberal" regime-type that Canada is placed in, along with
the United States and Australia. In this cluster:

> means-tested assistance, modest universal transfers, or modest
> social insurance plans predominate. These cater mainly to a
> clientele of low income, usually working class, state dependants.
> It is a model in which, implicitly or explicitly, the progress of
> social reform has been severely circumscribed by traditional,
> liberal work-ethic norms; one where the limits of welfare equal
> the marginal propensity to demand welfare instead of work.
> Entitlement rules are therefore strict and often associated with

---

[49] Esping-Andersen, "The Three Political Economies." See also Musynski's discussion in "Defending the welfare state," 317 ff.

[50] See Mullaly, "Social welfare" for an elaboration of these types.

stigma; benefits are usually modest. In turn, the state encourages the market, either passively by guaranteeing only a minimum, or actively by subsidizing private welfare schemes.

In this residual welfare type (using Titmuss's term), the state tries to arranges its benefit structure so that wages are always more attractive than benefits. It thus tends to reinforce a dual society, dividing regions and individuals into net donors and recipients of tax transfers, as well as dualizing labour markets into core and periphery segments (more on this later).

But it is in the main *ideological positions* on welfare that the duality in civil society is most fully elaborated and problematized. We look first at the traditional welfare paradigm and then the welfare rights approach. After this we review the restructuring of the Canadian welfare state that is now under way, partly under the guidance of a neo-conservative ideology.

Traditional Welfare Paradigm

As mentioned, the welfare state was conceived in the 1930s amidst social upheaval and human desperation. We saw that it took on its elite-driven residualist shape even in the teeth of a broad-based (but politically weak) social democratic constituency that wanted a full-employment welfare society. That being said, traditional welfare *ideology* provided (still does, for many) a blueprint for the construction of meaningful lives and careers in the service of the public. It also inscribes an *imaginary* scenario for Canada, invoking its unfulfilled potential as a caring and just nation that overcomes its distances and differences. In examining its roots, we are drawn to its moral content. Culpitt finds a wellspring of the welfare state in the "normative conjunction of the modern national state and the church."[51] The conception of the poor as children of God no less than anyone else, who possessed a simplicity and humility worthy of Christ's approval, dovetailed with the moral prescription that the good man gives alms to the poor. Equality of all the children of God, with their consequent human dignity, became a resonant theme of socially progressive Christianity. The Social Gospel, which conceived Christ's redemptive mission as in

---

[51] Culpitt, *Welfare and Citizenship*, 190. Both this author and Hewitt, *Welfare, Ideology and Need*, provide comprehensive analyses of welfare state ideologies and their conflicts.

large part the creation of a humane social order, infused the more liberal churches, whose members and ex-members were among the more influential social workers, reformers, researchers, civil servants, and political figures in the early welfare state. The socialist and Fabian traditions, more secular but no less morally directed, also organized the conceptions and activities of early welfare state reformers.

The dominant assumption of these reformers was that care of the disadvantaged was the obligation of those with skills and resources, whose "proxy" in carrying out these direct welfare responsibilities would be respective governments. What needed to be cultivated here was not a charitable heart, but rather a *social space* to which was ascribed forms of need and social right distinct from market space. The problems stemming from people's social and economic differences, the discriminatory advantages or deficits in educational or community services, the varying states of need of bodies and demographic categories — these elements of (what Foucault has called) the "biopolitical" were conceived to be within the purview of agents of, or parallel to, the state. A host of social specialists and clients soon peopled social space: welfare lawyers and legislators, social policy researchers and civil servants, social workers, helpers, counsellors, trainers, activists, and, of course, low-income people. The "social" became a field where services and goods were transferred, to be sure, but also where identities of helpers and helped could be realized and empowered, monitored and managed — in short, a field of power.

The shortcomings and critiques of the traditional welfare state and ideology soon revealed themselves. In contrast to its solidaristic rhetoric, the welfare state served particular class interests. The middle class garnered many of the benefits and jobs from welfare state expansion. Public sector bureaucrats, having little incentive to manage the delivery of services efficiently and at low cost, often indulged in empire-building — holding onto or expanding staff and resources whether or not they served a useful purpose. Furthermore, whether through occupational welfare on the job, or tax deductions for education and registered savings plans, welfare seemed a kind of subsidy of the middle-class lifestyle. (Ironically, according to Wolfe, "the new welfare state increasingly enables middle-class people to buy the labour of others who will perform their moral obligations for them."[52]) But if middle-class welfare benefits accrue from employment, is that not a recommodification of welfare, rooting it in individual market performance rather than social entitlement? If welfare aids the freedom of the individual to consume, then welfare and the social, having developed hand in hand, have separated, according to Squires's review of the British case. Only "the ideological symbols remain; *social* security, *national* health, ... echoes from a time when 'social' meant more than the aggregation of individuality."[53]

The welfare state and its ideology has been faulted for its paternalistic and bureaucratic authority. Women and minority groups (as well as Marxists, market liberals, and others) objected to the role and self-conception of government as the supreme guarantor of goods and services in the public interest. Social service professionals presented themselves as, and were thought to be, rational and impartial, but they wielded their considerable statutory and discretionary powers with an implicit paternalism: "We know what is best for you and you must accept it."[54] There was little dialogue with, or democratic participation of, individuals and communities. The critique was not of the welfare ideal but rather of "welfare statism," whose phalanx of political elites, analysts, managers and workers were neither conversant with nor accountable to the actual needs of living people to master their own circumstances. Furthermore, welfare officials seemed oblivious to the gender-biased, and racially discriminatory, aspects of their daily exercise of power.

Finally, some critics of the traditional welfare paradigm thought that it turned active citizens into passive expecters. Social democrats and socialists decried the neo-conservative assumption about the thoroughgoing individualism of people in society, instead calling individuals and groups to a struggle for a social citizenship of shared rights. But, as Wolfe writes, "the language of rights replaces one of

---

[52] Wolfe, *Whose Keeper?*, 156.

[53] Squires, *Anti-social Policy*, 44. His important quote hints at a substantive lessening of collective agency, solidarity, and purpose as Welfare becomes individualized and merely aggregative. Welfare is attacking social space.

[54] Culpitt, *Welfare and Citizenship*, 4.

obligations,"[55] and, once the goals are achieved, rights-bearers often become ethically non-responsive. But social citizenship is a contract between individuals and society, where a commitment to mutual rights and obligations to others is the correlative of received rights.

The traditional welfare paradigm carved out a social space, but one that was highly authoritative and structured. Its vision and ethical purpose was large, but in part professionally self-serving and class-guided. Two ideological alternatives emerged: a welfare rights approach which radicalized the traditional rights premise and wanted to expand decommodified social space, and a neo-conservative position which wanted commodifying market space to reassert its primacy over the social.

Welfare Rights Approach

In this approach, welfare is founded not on the obligation to care for the disadvantaged or the stranger, but, in Culpitt's words, "on the basis of the social legitimacy of the claim rights that various groups can espouse."[56] Three important elements in the above sentence define the welfare rights approach: the status of welfare rights, the issue of caring, and the group process involved. On the *status* of welfare rights the position is unequivocal. Welfare rights should be a part of a set of citizens' rights guaranteed by government, taking its place alongside the well-fortified political and legal rights.[57] Rights to welfare have the same weight as rights of property and they are to be legislated and enforced just as firmly.

Welfare is not about caring or compassion, which — when they replace justice in the public sphere — tend to be decadent. Ignatieff is quite clear:

> The language of citizenship is not properly about compassion at all, since compassion is a private virtue which cannot be legislated or enforced. The practice of citizenship is about ensuring everyone has the entitlements necessary to the exercise of their liberty.[58]

---

[55] Wolfe, *Whose Keeper?*, 183.

[56] Culpitt, *Welfare and Citizenship*, 190.

[57] Taylor-Gooby, *Social Change*, 21-22.

[58] Michael Ignatieff, cited in Culpitt, *Welfare and Citizenship*, 16.

In those instances where legitimate needs claims are severed from rights claims, the marginalized may find themselves cast as moralistic objects of the working out of (inappropriate) private virtue, or as the recipients of the paternalistic discretion of officials. Social space — for the welfare rightists — is a tough-minded, not tender-minded, domain, having more to do with levers of agency and structures of justice than feelings of brotherly love.

Finally, there is a constituting group process involved in the attainment of social rights. For radical critics such as Fraser, the making of social rights is not simply a top-down legislative or policy innovation, but a political struggle of marginal groups and their allies to translate "justified needs claims into social rights."[59] Women and minority thinkers/activists struggle against the old paternalism with its covert racism and sexism. Community groups in general often contest the whole professionalized, centralized, monological power structure of Wlfare. Why should outside policy analysts or social workers have the power to identify and meet needs, as though the community had no voice or relevant local knowledge? Why are detachment and objectivity more favoured virtues than community commitment and self-responsibility?[60] Community groups have developed locally based methods to ascertain and analyze their own needs and, in some cases, have intervened with their locally produced services. Democratization of social space, and the opportunity for citizens to be producers as well as recipients of services, are challenging traditional flows of influence and communication as well as the pretensions of "expert knowledge" itself.

Before we particularize too much here, we need to be reminded of the strengths of state welfare. Notwithstanding the welfare state's hegemonic means of controlling people and blunting their resistance, only the state can guarantee rights. Communities may change, private sector services may come and go, but statutory entitlements are founded in law, policy and government practice and they apply across the land. The welfare state, on balance, has prised open a decommodified space or arena for new political

---

[59] Fraser, "Struggle over needs," 183.

[60] Culpitt, *Welfare and Citizenship*, 56.

subjects to be formed. These subjects have spoken out to validate their claims to a level of non-market welfare provision needed to establish their just footing in society. In Hewitt's words, citing Laclau and Mouffe: "social subjects develop their own ideological project by extending the chain of equivalences between themselves and other subjects towards more democratic and egalitarian forms of political existence."[61]

Of course, there are criticisms of the welfare rights approach — for example., in its unchecked extension of social rights and in the profusion of claims-makers that populate the more permissive social space made available. If the rights paradigm becomes reified, there may be an implicit anarchism about social obligations beyond those of one's own group or community. The language of rights, Culpitt (arguably) contends, does not serve as a guide to the future because it (like that of the neo-conservatives)

> can only point to the defensive selfishness of a different pattern of strategic winning and playing. Thus the epistemology of welfare rights has to be seen as the "socially committed stand-points" of social administration.[62]

Powerful standpoints which guide political action or intellectual analysis will yield insight and meaningful praxis, but both the conduct of government *and* theoretical analysis requires that they be subsumed under a more general framework.

Neo-Conservatism and Welfare State Restructuring

The international economy faltered in the mid-1970s, due to the combination of inflationary pressures and economic downturns. The financing of the Vietnam war fuelled inflation, as did the oil crisis in the mid-East which quadrupled the price of oil. The Bretton Woods system of fixed exchange rates fell apart and the internationalizing of capital quickly built up productive activities in developing countries in excess of world demand. This prompted a shift to the right in the Anglo-Saxon liberal democracies, bringing us into the eighties with leaders such as Thatcher, Mulroney and

[61] Hewitt, *Welfare, Ideology and Need*, 140 — citing Laclau and Mouffe, *Hegemony and Socialist Structure*.

[62] Culpitt, *Welfare and Citizenship*, 185.

Reagan. This neo-conservative rise had two major parts, for our purposes: it tilted government concern *towards* trying to balance the budget and control inflation and *away from* the ongoing governmental support for the unemployed and disadvantaged.

Ideological shifts aside, the actual material cuts to social spending in the last decade have been profound. Looking at all the G7 countries (Canada, France, Italy, Japan, UK, United States, West Germany), there have been declines in the growth of public spending on welfare programs, the real value of benefits, and the ratio of unemployment benefit to earnings. The biggest cuts have occurred in the liberal capitalist democracies which have been most influenced by the new right (Canada, Britain, the U.S., New Zealand). The result for Britain, with the neediest getting the most serious cuts in a system that broadly remained intact, has been aptly termed "implosion," which is a bursting within.[63] Here are some of Canada's implosive cuts in recent years:

- amendment of the Unemployment Insurance Act by withdrawing the federal contribution to the fund, lengthening the waiting period and shortening the duration of benefits in many parts of the country; also net cuts to training;

- clawbacks to family allowances and Old Age Security from people with yearly incomes of $50,000 or more — which has reduced the whole notion of universality of benefits which has been a pillar of Canadian public policy;[64]

- capping, in 1989, federal cost-share payments to the Canada Assistance Plans for three provinces; then the federal decision to discontinue CAP program altogether by 1996, replacing it with block grants to provinces for health, education and welfare. This will decentralize welfare funding, reduce its rules and national standards, and cut up to $7 billion from these portfolios in two years;

- partial de-indexation of family allowances and child tax credits which has meant that the proportional increase of the tax burden between 1984 and 1991 was greatest for the poor

---

[63] Taylor-Gooby, *Social Change*, 4.

[64] Mullaly, "Social welfare," 83.

and less as you go up the income ladder. It has resulted in $3.5 billion less going to low-income Canadians;[65]

- as one provincial example in 1995, Ontario's severe reduction of legal aid funding, its cutting of the non-profit co-operative housing program, its threatened cuts to the drug plans for welfare poor and seniors, and its planned removal of rent control; and, finally,

- Ontario's cutting of welfare benefits across the board by 21 percent, to move the province's benefit level to 10 percent above the national average — while promising a substantial tax cut to the province's better-off taxpayers.

As mentioned earlier (p.12), less than half of Canadians without jobs (49.7 percent) now qualify for Unemployment Insurance (UI) benefits, down from 83 percent before the Mulroney and Chretien governments began their cuts in 1989. Those who manage to get on UI need to work longer for payments which are smaller and last for shorter periods. As a result, Canada's UI system is one of the least generous among the industrial nations.[66]

The government is privatizing some of its services, contracting them out to business and the voluntary sector. New assumptions are in play, one of them being that governments can never answer as sensitively and efficiently to social uncertainties and shifts in demand as private service providers can.[67] Devolution is occurring as well, as the source of services shifts downward from the federal and provincial governments to municipal governments; then, due to the inadequacy of public funding, to the voluntary agencies, the food banks, and, finally, families. The two developments of privatization and devolution, even somewhat accelerated by the centrifugal force of constitutional demands, are bringing us back in time, Yalnizyan notes, reversing the evolution of social security that started in the 1930s.[68] The conclusion of Mullaly seems appropriate: "the new right is moving the welfare state away from the notion of

---

[65] Yalnizyan, "Securing society," 43-44.

[66] *CCPA Monitor*, July-August, 1995, 12.

[67] Culpitt, *Welfare and Citizenship*, 7.

[68] Yalnizyan, "Securing society," 45.

citizenship (equality of entitlement) to one of class (inequality of entitlement). It will also be argued that this restructuring removes several restrictions to capital accumulation."[69]

The Study

This research grew out of a desire to know how low-income people were coping in London, Ontario, in the late eighties. We felt that the best way of learning this was to conduct in-depth interviews in people's homes. Knowing that the poor are drawn into interactions with public officials and service providers, we thought it necessary to interview a sampling of these latter groups as well. The hope was that this triangulated approach would more accurately portray low-income people and service-providers within the field of their interactions and negotiations.

Within an essentially convenience sample, nineteen low-income individuals were interviewed. They were approached informally in various community settings, usually within the low-income area of Dundas Street, east of Adelaide. We widened the recruitment somewhat by advertizing in community newspapers. The sampling aim was to canvas a wide range of kinds of people and situations: working poor, those on assistance, male and female, young and old. For the service providers (eighteen in number), the aim was to find a mixture of organizations: governmental and non-governmental organizations, those established and those striving for legitimacy, religious and non-religious. We wanted to make sure that a wide range of services and goods were offered within our sampling. The main research tool was the open-ended but focused interview, lasting from one to three hours. When permitted, the interviews were taped and later transcribed. While certain questions were asked of everyone — in both samples — the sequence of question and answer was fitted to the narrative flow of the informants.

What is the nature of the transactions in this social services/action field (SSA)? Pure exchange considerations would not seem, on the surface, to apply: in measurable material terms, the poor do not

---

[69] Mullaly, "Social welfare," 80.

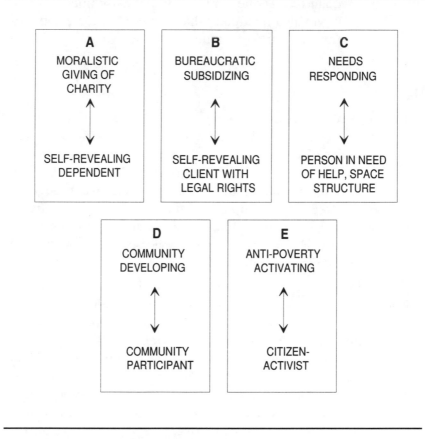

Figure 1: *Typology of Role Configurations for Service Providers*

pay back their givers. But, in a different sense, they do. The interview accounts suggest that what the service providers and organizations want from the recipients is the enactment of a role, the performance of which is aimed at helping the poor but also validating the organization. But the concept of role needs to be elaborated in its relational dynamics. It is actually a role configuration, which consists of the linking of the self-conception and presentation by the service provider, with the accorded definition held out to the low-income recipient. "This is what we are and do, and this is what you are and do in our presence." Indeed, even more than an accorded definition, the service provider proffers a mode of self-relation to the recipient.

In fact, the organization is one constitutive part of a field of relations which the person enters when he has low income and has expressed need. Now the low-income person has not the power to configure the other in such an authoritative way, but is not reduced to simply fitting into the sociological forms held out to him. The low-income person plays the role with varying commitment, depending partly on belief and partly on a calculus of self-interest and self-protection. This book looks at the encounter between role configurations constructed by the service providers and the responding and proactive practices of low-income recipients as they cope with poverty and the social forms of the service providers.

The interviews with service providers suggest that organization/recipient relations are structured in at least five different role configurations (see Figure 1), which will be presented in chapters 3 to 7. The range is from a self-exposing dependent dealing with a moralizing giver of charity at one side, to an active, politicized citizen joining in a struggle with fellow citizens on the other. Low-income people must choose among the various role configurations "on offer" in the hope of minimizing the cost to the self, while still meeting his or her needs for assistance. Their coping strategies in market society are explored in Chapter 2, while the responsive and transformative practices they engage in vis à vis the social services/action field take up Chapter 8.

2

"Making Do" in A Market Society

*I*n March 1976, the number of people on welfare was 1.3 million, while in 1993 the figure was almost three million. Most analysts conclude that the higher rates of unemployment are the main factor in the marked increase in the number of people on UI and welfare in recent times. This may be illustrated by research done by the Department of Social Services in London, Ontario. In March, 1994, the city's Canada Employment Centre reported 1,957 job vacancies in London. In that same month 42,933 individuals or heads of households were on UI and welfare: 14,644 individuals on UI, 14,745 heads of households on city welfare, and 13,544 heads of households on provincial welfare. While some of the welfare households were headed by people who were not employable, others had more than one employable adult.[70]

With regard to incomes, there has been a polarization in recent years. Government policies such as taxation and transfers moderate the growing inequality of market incomes, but not very much. The bottom three quintiles of income earners lost income shares during the last decade. Put in dollar terms, between 1981 and 1991, upper-income families increased their proportion of Canada's total income at the cost of middle- and low-income families. The total distribution was valued at around $5.4 billion.[71] The record of market incomes alone in the prevention of poverty is dismal. If it were not for government transfers, the bottom decile of income earners would have to exist on virtually no income at all.[72] As for that most common of poverty incomes, the minimum wage, it has

---

[70] National Council of Welfare, *A Blueprint*, 30.

[71] Ross, Shillington, and Lochhead, *Canadian Fact Book*, 47.

[72] Ibid., 92.

declined in real value since 1975 by up to 30 percent, depending on the province.[73]

Of course, there are other factors that produce poverty: unequal sharing of household and family duties, marriage breakdown, inadequate social benefits, and low educational attainment. But it must be stressed that the poor record of market earnings, along with unemployment and underemployment, have been principal contributors.

Daily Needs and Resources

With that general context in mind, what is the basic material situation of poor people, and how is that reflected in their self-described daily experiences in the marketplace? Though brief mention will be made of the wider societal deprivations imposed on them, the portrait the informants draw is full of the concrete details that poverty forces them to be mindful of. We start with a basic question: how much money do low-income people have at their disposal each day? And how does that level of resources prepare one for participation in the moneyed world beyond the social services network: i.e., in labour and housing markets and in shopping for food and clothes? After recounting the struggles for the basics, we look at the vitally important activity of working, not just for pay but in the domestic realm of parent and child. Finally we focus on the universals of poverty experience. There is the feeling of being pulled by the strings of contingency, which evokes a strategic-adaptive manner of manipulating self and resources; and there is the sense of being immobile and isolated, which prompts a careful and selective social participation.

Consider a day in the life of a poor person, in material terms.[74] According to surveys for 1991, an average poor urban family of two adults and two children (and bringing it up to the 1994 cost of living) receives a daily dollar amount for each member of *$14.60* — which totals $21,300 annually. The daily per-person expenditure estimate for food (drawing from the Department of Agriculture's

[73] Musynski, "A new social welfare," 182.

[74] Ross, Shillington, and Lochhead, *Canadian Fact Book*, 3.

Thrifty Nutritious Food Plan) is $4.75. The daily per-person esti-
mated cost for shelter (based on Canada Mortgage and Housing
Corporation data) is $7.16. And the daily per-person estimated cost
for clothing (based on the Montréal Diet Dispensary) is $1.22. Taken
together, the daily costs of the essentials for survival in Canada
amounts to $13.13. Out of the *$1.47* per person per day that is left,
families must pay their phone bill, transportation, recreation and
entertainment, household expenses, personal care items, insurance,
medicines, books and school supplies, and on and on. The brutal
constraint imposed by having so little money in a complex moneyed
society shapes most of life, externally and in one's psyche. It drives
people to cut down on food intake and quality, to go to food banks
and soup kitchens, to depend on family members, and to sell their
possessions. Internally, it leads them to doubt their own self-worth,
to disbelieve in their future, and to express their anger and sense
of rejection internally and within their relationships.

The marketplace that many poor people enter is structured so as
to increase the probability of their unsuccess. Because of such
factors as age, inexperience, disability, or lack of educational
credentials, applicants are rejected by employers and thus deprived
of a means of livelihood (the state having retreated from job
creation). Many people are unable to afford the training and time
to re-fit themselves for new skill demands. They many find themselves on a treadmill of minimum wage or non-standard jobs that
guarantees their poverty. Still others, often women, find themselves
bound to family responsibilities after a marriage break-up, and so
unable to gain a foothold in the occupational or educational
spheres. Within the welfare state, these transitional and/or dependent states were decommodified — that is, they were provided for
in a form of welfare other than market provision. Even more, people
came to believe that, under circumstances of economic disadvantage, they had *rights* to non-market goods and services. What the
new right's retrenchment of the welfare state is achieving is to tilt
the emphasis back to commodification, where it is performance in
the market that decides one's fate.[75] This increases the power of the
employer and makes the low wages they offer to the disadvantaged

---

[75] Mullaly, "Social welfare."

applicant (in the secondary labour market) more determinative of life chances.

So the market that the poor enter now is less and less mediated by welfare entitlement and safety net; it is more naked in its power relations and costs. How does the marketplace configure persons who enter it? What modes of self-relation are fostered? People are constructed as calculating, self-interested competitors on a market for the obtaining of personal wants. The market constructs possessive individualists, whose own and family's and company's interest takes precedence over the organization of society as a provider of justice for all. The partisans of the market want to defend its primacy as *the* arena for human struggle (with charity for the losers). It is in the market where the heroes will emerge, where the greatest endeavours and human stories will be played out, where the life chances of all will be determined. The market will brook no rivals in the establishment of wages or entitlements. Social wages and benefits will be stripped down so as to end their superiority over the lowest market wage, which will have the effect of pushing welfare claimants into the market. The conception of a good society where all have rights and duties and parts to play, irrespective of market attainment, is being replaced by a conception of an individualistic society where the market assigns the parts, entitlements and rewards.

Struggling for the Basics: "Making Do"

Buying and Managing Food

In 1989, it took $115 a week to feed balanced and nutritious meals to a family of four. But that same family on welfare had less than $500 a month to spend on essentials after the rent was paid. Balanced meals, then, are almost impossible, particularly at the end of the month.[76] Indeed, food is often what is sacrificed when the poor are confronted with unforeseen inflexible expenses. As an instance, George needed to move from St. Thomas to London to pursue a training course in the mental health field at a community college. On a fixed income (Vocational Rehabilitation), he was not

---

[76] Dahlia Reich, "Nutritious meals," C2.

given extra for moving expenses. When asked about the food situation for himself, his non-working wife and two children, he responded:

> This month? [laughs] It's a little rough ... We had to rent a truck in order to get here, which cost $200, so it had to come out of someplace. So once the bills were paid, your food money was left ... We've got about $80 left in the bank, to last us for the rest of the month. So this month, I can see it being kinda tight.

Back when he was "busing it" from St. Thomas, Vocational Rehab helped him with the fare and, in his words, "it didn't mean that I was going to be taking food off the table." Food, being an extremely flexible item, is, not surprisingly, the focus of endless strategic consideration. We turn now to food shopping.

In the consumer marketplace — the predominant source of food — the informants alternated strategically between mainstream and down-market food stores, seeking relentlessly for affordable "soft spots" in the spectrum of outlets. While shopping at the A&P or IGA, they would buy the cheaper cuts of beef, the utility grade chicken parts, the chunk bologna, the bruised fruit, the staler items. They would search for sales and specials, and use coupons. The informant who had managed to secure a freezer, perhaps from a relative or with the tax refund, counted herself lucky. Having a freezer allowed Stephanie to buy all her groceries at once, usually when her Mother's Allowance cheque arrived.

The poverty-wise were rigorously practical in their stratagems — Which stores are closest to the bus and have the best specials? What are the basics: milk, bread, lunch meat for the kids, etc.? What are the coupons for and how much will it cost me to travel to the various stores? In summer, drinks are needed. "After that I try to cover the basic food groups. Whatever I can afford," Nancy indicated. Albert, a single father, wants fresh vegetables for his family, but when a head of lettuce goes up 29 cents he cannot afford it. He tends to pass over vegetables and fruits because "I don't like the kids guzzling them up ... Like if I buy a bag of apples, I want that bag of apples to last ... and I can't really afford to buy something that's going to be gone in two days." He tried once to make a food budget, with lists of what they need to eat, but

> what I need and what I absolutely have to have are two different things. So usually what gets bought is what we absolutely have to have.

So he buys the things that last: cereals, cheese, hamburgers, macaroni, hot dogs. People freeze their milk, buy cheap white bread and, in single mother Michele's words, "if you're lucky you survive until baby bonus, which comes near the end of the month, and then you go shop again for the last week of the month."

This disciplined balancing act — of transportation, money, nutrition, time — depends on keeping other expenses at bay. When these dreaded expenses do appear, people go hungry, or substitute sandwiches for hot meals, or eat starchy foods that fill the stomach, or go to the Food Bank or a relative. People talk of being drained of energy. Dan and Sandra, a poor couple superintending a public housing complex, remember eating porridge for a week and popcorn for three days. Kevin was in a mass layoff at Algoma Steel in Sault Ste. Marie and the unemployment office could not process 6000 or 7000 workers fast enough. While awaiting his "pogey" (Unemployment Insurance), he lived mainly off what he could cook from a few bags of rolled oats. When we asked Michele if she was eating well, she said, "No I won't say that. For example, this morning I had a bowl of soup and a couple pieces of bread. I had Kraft dinner yesterday." She finds fruits and vegetables and whole wheat bread expensive, but manages to keep her children in apples and fruit juice. Generally, though, they eat a lot of potatoes, rice and pasta. Combining these with ground beef, she claims she can make a meal for under three dollars.

The Social Meanings of Distributing Food

When food is scarce, the provision of food to others changes its pattern and meaning. One informant pointed out that the reason Christmas is such a burden to the poor (and drives them to the food bank afterwards) is not only that they must find money for gifts, but that they must entertain family members who "don't realize," according to Stephanie, "that, when you're on Mother's Allowance, you're on a low income. You don't have groceries. And it's hard for people to just come over to visit; you know, they want a coffee or tea and it gets expensive after a while." So, lacking the money for food to entertain others, the response of the poor person is to cut down on social life and withdraw (selectively) from friends. Unlike older societies when people grew their own food and, when a guest appeared, threw another potato on the turf fire, in our society visitors are a problem for a resource-poor family, and indeed can cause feelings of shame.

The single mothers tend to feed their children better than themselves, and this pattern needs description and interpretation. After telling of the poor quality of the food she eats ("garbage foods, junk foods"), Michele was asked, Does this quality of eating affect your four-year old son? Her answer was no, "because he is getting what he needs, I'm not. I eat totally differently than he does." She eats once or twice a day and her son eats three times. He gets his dietary requirements and she does not. She fears that if she drinks milk, there will not be enough for him throughout the month. She abstains from cereal, because it takes milk, and instead eats bread and eggs; but, since he gets most of the eggs, Michele ends up eating toast. Similarly, another single mother, Nancy, answers the question, Do I feel I'm eating well? in this way: "Well, the kids are. They may not like eating all their veggies, but they do eat them. They get their fruit one way or the other." She goes on to say, significantly, "they're healthy, so that must mean something. Me, lately, I haven't felt like eating too much of anything." When they get tomato juice, she gratefully seizes on it and claims it as "mine. The kids hate it [laughs]. So I'm OK there."

Stephanie, a single mother on Mother's Allowance, gives us a key to understanding the sacrificial pattern of the single mothers. Her parents were middle-class and worked all their lives. Even though her poverty was not self-generated — her ex-husband was an alcoholic and a sexual abuser of her children — she has come to view her poverty with a strong sense of *guilt*.

> You probably will find that with a lot of your moms out there. So very guilty, that ... I'm the one who had these children. It's all my fault ... I'm the one who had these kids. I'm the one who took on having sex with my husband ... and knew what the consequences were. And if you take the responsibility for having a child, then you also take on the responsibility of caring for that child and supporting them.

Then, in the same breath, she challenges the self-responsible interpretation with a more contextual account: "But when you have three kids and you can't get out and work because the income wouldn't allow you, you need to have that backup system. And my parents cannot afford to back me up." So her ending up "on the system" is so shameful to her parents' daughter that her situational critique loses force. She is emphatic: "The money that I get that comes in, goes into my house and my children — I don't take it for myself." Later, describing a therapist's advice to take care of herself first, Stephanie disagrees: "Your children are always right there. They're the ones that need the food in their mouths."

To not eat their just deserts of the publicly provided food is to express their non-entitlement to benefits. There is, of course, a self-esteem accruing from giving to the children, but it does not make up for the wasting away of these mothers' sense of entitlement to *anything* for the work they are doing and the persons they are. This may be the result of a twofold patriarchal message. First of all, she does not think the benefits are for her. After all, the public system has enclaved her and her kind, seeming to look past her to the children, as if she were their mere caretaker, preparing them for society and state. Secondly, by not partaking of her share of the benefits, she is showing her acquiescence in capitalism's valuation of her parenting work. Capitalist society enshrines a fundamental exchange: we put in work time to get our rewards. This equation privileges employment over other forms of work — for example, domestic labour. The money from Mother's Allowance is not felt to be connected to an exchange for her parenting labour, so does not belong to the recipient, who feels guilty taking it and only spends it in particular ways.

Coping with Housing

Urban housing development configures city places into commercial properties and real estate, thus ejecting the poor from homes, flats and neighbourhoods in the central city. (Poor people need to be near shops and services, because transportation and even the telephone is expensive for them.) Developers find it more profitable to build condominiums for the better-off than low-income housing. In addition, there is the encroachment of upper-income "gentrifiers" who move into an older neighbourhood and eventually have the effect of pricing the poor out of their communities. On the rental market, the requirement of first and last months' rent screens out poor people. As well, what the market does not screen out, apartment finders do. Landlords contract out for the services of apartment-finders, who agree to screen out poor single parents, ex-mental patients, and especially the unemployed. As a result of this exclusion, according to Chris (a service provider in the sample, working for access to housing), low-income people often turn to crime — prostitution, break and entry — simply to afford rent.

There is a view afoot that most of Canada's poor people are adequately housed; i.e., that they receive generous shelter allowances, or are in public housing, and that a good number own their homes free and clear. This is not true. Only 12 percent of the working-age poor under 65 owned their homes outright in 1991. In the same year, only 19 percent of poor people receive a rental subsidy of some kind.[77] The subsidy is rarely enough; most rents in London are often significantly higher than the maximum Welfare pays for rent. Sixty percent of social assistance recipients will pay more rent than the Welfare allowance provides. As for public housing, only 10 percent of all social assistance recipients live in it.[78] As for the informants in our study, roughly one-third lived in government subsidized housing, another third lived in rental units, and the rest were in non-profit housing co-operatives, living with parents or siblings, and one person was paying a mortgage on her own home. (We will leave the experience of public housing to the chapter on receiving and acting, since the focus of this chapter is on market situations.)

There is a dearth of low-cost rental housing that is dispersed in middle- and upper-class communities, largely due to a kind of residential segregation (one author calls it "residential apartheid"[79]). High housing prices serve as a kind of barrier to the lower-income person, but more important are zoning laws forbidding the building of apartments in houses. Ontario has been the first province to legalize these apartments in July 1994, thus allowing people who are under economic strain to find a way to keep their houses, and giving poor tenants a chance to live in an unsegregated neighbourhood. Residential zoning is, in effect, people zoning and has been the instrument of the better-off to keep the poor, mental patients, special-needs groups, immigrants and single mothers out. Not only does it keep the poor out, it contributes to the ghettoization of the

----

[77] Ross, Shillington, and Lochhead, *Canadian Fact Book*, 7-8.

[78] Ad Hoc Collective, "Some cuts don't heal."

[79] Hulchanski, "Ontario's blow."

poor in undesirable parts of the city. The isolation of the poor, and their greater visibility, not only shows disrespect, but actively encourages it. Social distance leads to rumours and stereotypes about the isolated. As Miller writes, "Segregation makes access to jobs more difficult both in terms of transportation difficulties and isolation from useful networks of information and contacts. The result is that the jobless segregated are more easily characterized as unwilling to work."[80]

The market accommodation of the poor is often squalid and insecure. It is difficult to take pride in the place that, no matter what you do, you cannot keep clean. Cooking odours of other families drift into the house and the noise and intrusiveness of neighbours invade privacy. The corridors, in some cases, are unsafe to walk through. If the building is owned by speculators, there is the fear that the building will be torn down, or that tenants will be evicted. Despite this, informants generally indicated a preference for decent, unadministered, affordable market housing over public housing. (The exception would be those, such as Stephanie and Kevin, who are living more or less contentedly in non-profit co-operative housing.) This preference is a costly one, however. Judith, a single mother with two children, lives in a normal rental unit, but pays about 80% of her income on rent (not unusual). Other, such as Brenda, sacrifice enormously to have a market apartment for her and her two sons, because she does not want public housing. She pays $300 a month more for her apartment than she paid for public housing, and suffers for it — but at least has the pleasure of living in an apartment of the type she used to clean.

Finally, living in your own space after a life of poverty is experienced as a kind of arrival and a blessing. Nowhere is this more poignantly illustrated than in Ann's case. She is a woman, over seventy, who worked all her life. She has worked in restaurants, washing dishes and pots and pans and doing short order work from 2 p.m. to 2 a.m., with a 15-minute break. She has worked with heavy presses in the laundry business, has done house-cleaning, has handed out coupons at Miracle Mart, and has looked after her mother-in-law before she went into a nursing home. Though

---

[80] Miller, "Poverty and respect," 21.

earning some years between $12 and $14 a week, she managed to raise four children on her own.

Her pride is strong. Asked whether she had ever received food from a food bank or soup kitchen, Ann answered, "No, no, I've always been independent." She acquired a home with her second husband, now dead, and with some short-term financial support from her adult children, still lives in it. She talks about the house as if it were somehow her life, solidified in community form. "I've worked, and everything I've done, and that my second husband did, was in this house. This is mine." Her determination to work, not to be "down and out," was fuelled by her fervent desire to "have my own place, my own furniture that I worked for." Underneath the static cover of her dead-end jobs pulsed the energy of her personal resolve — which had enabled her to endure her work and her poverty.

She has made her children aware that this home is where she will live, not in a nursing home. "When I get old enough, I'm going to [still] have my own house. I'm not going to be paying someone else's rent." Ann's home is the symbol of her entitlement, the validation of her hard life, and the centre that her self inhabits. Her desire for her own home is the desire for a stable place in the community, an independent status, a fastness in the swirling tumult of the marketplace. But the financial help provided by her children towards the mortgage is shakier now and less regular, due to their own financial difficulties. So, once again, the predictable happens: a poor person finds herself facing insecurity.

Handling Clothes and Personal Appearance

The presentation of self at school, on the dating scene, and in so many interactions with others requires clothes that are new and in fashion. Not to wear these clothes, which are the uniform of the conventional, is to signal to others that you are different and that you are poor. For children especially, to wear old clothes is to risk being ridiculed at school. So Albert spoke of his son coming home from school "all upset because some kid at school rode him about his clothes. 'What Goodwill store did you get them out of?'" Clothes bought from the Thrift shop make budgetary sense for the parent, but do not meet the expressive and status needs of the children. Single mothers, in particular, are riven by the conflict between the need to hold onto money and the strong want of their children for trendy new running shoes.

At the adult level, informants found that their clothes affected their reception on the job market. Beth, a single woman struggling up from lifelong poverty, had worked for years as a waitress and in other marginal jobs. She has been slowly upgrading her education and wanted a responsible job working with people. Such a job posting appeared in a local hospital. "I got myself together," Beth said, "and made an appointment to fill out an application. I went down looking as best as I could manage, though my clothing situation was very bleak." The employer looked at her and said, "You must be the one here for the janitorial position." Beth was devastated by the words. Her clothes sent out a class signal that was received as: You are not the person we want, but are one of those people who will take anything.

Kevin is very knowledgeable about the symbolic cues of used clothing. Growing up poor, he is used to wearing hand-me-down clothing. He has not bought a new shirt or pair of pants for three or four years, so his clothes are not in fashion. In current years it has been less of a problem, due to the tolerance for odd clothing in the punk scene. But in quiet bars, he feels the gaze of others taking in his class markers and making judgment:

> they take a look at you, and won't even talk to you, because you look like you don't make enough money to buy yourself some new clothes in three or four years. So why would they get to know you? You couldn't buy them a beer. *And they're right.* (emphasis added)

You cannot hide your situation. "As much as you try to keep ahead of it, there's no way." You go for half a year without a haircut, because you cannot afford it, and people notice. Then, when you get a haircut, "you look like: you can finally afford a haircut [chuckles]. You got the tan lines run down your forehead and down your face."

Kevin's view of why he thinks "they're right" to shun him is his sad and rueful observation that no one wants to know poor people. No one wants to hear their hard stories. Kevin goes out with a girl for a drink, then pools his scarce dollars together for dinner, then cannot afford to call her for a month or so. She finally gets the message that he is poor (at least that is his interpretation of why she does not call). But he applies the same calculative judgment in his relations with women. He notices the single women who take care of their clothes and look like they are not hurting financially, but he knows. Having grown up with mended clothing, "you can see, without actually trying to look for it, you can see the people who repaired that skirt for the fourth or fifth time, as opposed to those who haven't." Nobody says anything, but nobody wants to form a relationship with them. You "hope to meet someone who's got money, [then] you try to like that person as much as you can. It's terrible, but that's the way it is." If he met a woman who was making $30-40,000 a year, he would try to like her as much as he could. Every date and relationship is gauged, in part, for its monetary potential — in a kind of erotic stratification model.

Obsessed about class symbolism, Kevin verges on distortion. His comments on riding the bus are a case in point:

> Anyone who rides the bus [chuckles] doesn't have money. Right there. Anybody who can afford a car will gladly drive to work, even if it costs them more than the bus. They want to show that they have the money, they want to show off.

Kevin is bothered by conspicuous consumption, and imputes a petty, exhibitionistic intent to those who drive cars. Similarly, he ascribes poverty to all bus-riders. In another interpretation, he thinks all those who eat at mall restaurants with daily specials are "financially not-so-great off. There's all sorts of little things you can pick up on." Why is his world coloured in such binary, poor/non-poor hues? Perhaps the humiliated develop a fine-tuned sensitivity to pick up the subtle indicators of a pariah status amidst affluent society. Perhaps, as well, Kevin uses this sensitivity as an adaptive strategy so that, when the break comes, he can look as little like a loser as possible.

Modes of Working: At Home and on the Job

Parenting

Raising children under the conditions of poverty can be a sorrowing and stressful experience. Dan recalls his parents crying on each other's shoulders when they were just too overwhelmed for words. They may have been crying over how difficult it is to preside over the stunting of the lives of their children. Drawing on current knowledge, consider the ways poor children stand out in relation to their more affluent peers:

> they are less healthy, have less access to skill-building activities, have more destructive habits and behaviours, live more stressful lives and are subject to more humiliation. In short, they have less stable and less secure existences and as a result are likely to be less secure as adults.[81]

As compared with non-poor peers, poor children are more likely to smoke, to perform poorly in school and to drop out, to use drugs, to have an alcohol problem, and to have a psychiatric disorder.

Parenting, especially for the single parents of children under school age, can be unrelenting responsibility and burden, but also exacting and satisfying *work*. The burden of children is their inescapable *there-ness*, their needfulness and dependency. Their concerns crowd out adult self-concerns and projects. Being the hope for a better, uncontaminated future, children draw a strong emotional investment from their parents and preferential treatment as regards food and clothing. Parents want to be strong for their children and protect them from the impacts of poverty. Parents will undergo enormous sacrifices to shield their children from the stigma that comes from not having the right clothes or transportation. Brenda is cleaning houses illegally (making income unreported to Mother's Allowance) in part to afford her apartment, but also to provide her children with bus passes so that they can be their normal, active, teenage selves.

Stephanie is taking university courses partly to show an example to her children. She is not only living her own life but also (in a sense) her children's lives in prospect.

> And a lot of kids are depressed because the mother cannot handle it. But if the mom can stay strong, and if the mom can get out and work and do something for herself and be happy — those kids are going to see that, and they're going to grow up and be just like that. But if they keep getting cut down and don't get out there, those kids are going to grow up to be just like their mom.

She has to be strong for them, and that adds to her own strength and determination. She also, however, has a great need for parent relief from time to time and is almost poetic about the freedom of

---

[81] Ross, Shillington, and Lochhead, *Canadian Fact Book*, 2.

these child-free times. This brings us to the broader issue of the lack of affordable child care for poor parents so that they can pursue individual goals as training and job search. Child care is by no means common for poor children: it is estimated in a 1988 survey that only 5 percent of all poor children under age 13 (and 8 percent of those under age 6) live in families that received partial or full government child care subsidies.[82] What happens is that poor parents pay baby-sitters or have family members help out. Stephanie, whose extended family lives in Ottawa, expressed the constraint well: "[R]ight now any time I walk out of the house without my kids, it costs me money. Sounds terrible, but it does. You have to pay for a baby-sitter because there's not somebody else here."

For all the frustrations, mostly parenting is a complex, multi-faceted piece of work. Albert, the single father, takes pride in his parenting. He goes to classes, support groups, and tries disciplinary strategies. For his daughter, he has enlisted the help of Big Sisters. He is quick to take offence at the suggestion of some people that it was inappropriate for him to be a stay-at-home dad (one person even suggesting that his children be put up in a foster home!).

Employment Experiences

The jobs available for many lower-income people are service proletarian jobs, characterized by poor wages and benefits, insecurity, temporary status, with little training or career advancement. If escape from this secondary labour market into secure employment is not probable, the average worker, according to Esping-Andersen, "will likely face a poverty carousel: moving between low-paid jobs and various forms of social assistance, all depending on the business cycle and other forces beyond individual control."[83] The poorly paid jobs on offer do not compel any commitment, nor do they form the foundation of any future-directed project. The failure of market income, especially at the minimum wage level, to prevent worsening poverty, and to sustain the purchasing power of the poorer income-earners, has been noted in Chapter 1. One of the informants, John, attested to this critique of market incomes. The cause

---

[82] Ibid., 8.

[83] Esping-Andersen, "Labour movements," 58.

of poverty, in his view, was "the inequity of the way wealth is shared." An income of six or seven dollars an hour is like a stagnant pond. It offers no incentive to get off social assistance, nor does it given any hope of rising to "jobs in the middle range of ten to twelve dollars an hour [which] are very difficult to come by."

Before describing the working conditions of informants on marginal jobs, we should inquire what the informants *wanted* out of a job. After experiencing close supervision and hassles from employers, both Peter and John wanted jobs where they could be proud of themselves. Peter wanted a job where, the better he did, the more he proved to himself what he could do. John wanted a workplace where people did not work for and with strangers, where everyone knew everyone, and you naturally treated people well. John's communitarian position shone through when he was asked what he got out of his current work (helping maintain rental units for a man he liked, but for low pay):

> the feeling that I am part of the community. Knowing that I am
> helping someone accomplish his goals, maintenance and upkeep
> of rental dwellings. It feels good to help out, besides the money.

The *actual* working conditions which the informants described were harsh. To be poor in a marginal job is to confront the will-to-power of others without the protection of one's own (or a union's) countervailing power. Relations with employers can be up-close, abrasive and pressuring. Peter described a boss who "liked to insult people. I put up with it for three months. Then I came to the decision. I was either going to deck the guy or change jobs. I changed jobs. Wouldn't look good on a resume: 'decked Assistant Manager.'" On another job with a youth project, he was assigned to work in a kitchen that was so hot and unventilated that workers fainted.

Daniel, in his fifties, has found low-level jobs exploitative and demeaning. Instead of a regular routine of expected duties, he found himself used as a "gofer": running for this man to get this, for that man to get that, finding them a bucket of water, etc. He was hired by one company for floor maintenance, which he expected to do, but they were badgering him with tasks in the garbage area. In his job search, Daniel has had doors slammed in his face and has been told by employers to "f___ off." Sandra, his partner, has reported that he has returned from the job search broken-hearted and depressed.

We will look at Kevin's case in more detail. He had worked for Algoma Steel, whose union had pressured the company to ensure the workers' safety. His next (and current) job was working for a large, non-union, photography chain, in which unsafe practices were common. With a year of medical laboratory technology behind him, he knew the dangers of working with acids and toxins. The company had him working in conditions where he was sticking his arms up to his shoulders in silver toxin waste. As a result, he was physically run down and had sores. He claimed that the company cut corners and did not fully follow the latest worker safety legislation. Cyanide gas is produced from the removal of excess silver from the pictures and, in a unventilated back room behind the lab, people got quite sick. The job is more or less transient: people come in, are trained minimally and not expected to last more than a few years. To make a career of it would be foolish. Supervisors and managers do not make enough to justify the responsibility and the risk.

Indifferent to its workforce and its development and safety, the company pours its surplus into lavish advertising and its several mall outlets and labs. The wages are exploitative. For a time Kevin was running a warehouse for the company, which entailed supplying the goods, the chemical paper, and the other supplies for all the labs in London. For all the ordering, shipping, receiving and handling of hazardous goods, he was making $800 a month gross. He wanted badly to retrain, but since the company does not lay off, he would have to quit. That would force a 6-week delay before he would be eligible for retraining. He describes himself as being "between a rock and a hard place." Too proud to have Welfare take care of him, he stays on at the photo company.

Common Elements of Poor Experience

Along with the differences in poor experience, there are strong commonalities. To be poor is to be caught up in contingencies. As well, to be poor is to be relatively immobile and isolated, but yet still seeking a community close at hand.

Contingency

"Contingent" outcomes are those that depend on the actions of other individuals, or the availability of resources, or the operation of systems. It is our lot as humans to experience contingency, but to the poor it is a daily constant. Like marionettes, they are entangled by the strings of others: the physical, concrete exigencies of ordinary life, the unrelieved burdens of children, the scheduling demands of part-time employers, the obstacles due to immobility and isolation, the waiting and queuing on the telephone and in reception areas. For low-income people even simple tasks are labour- and time-intensive, requiring a closely focused attention to practical details. Depending on others forces a mindfulness about the needs and rules imposed by the people on whom one depends.

When material resources are stretched so thin, one walks on eggshells hoping some problem will not spring up and yank you in an unanticipated direction. As a small example, Louise's vacuum cleaner broke down. She had to fix it for $100, the motor having burned out. "With the carpet, you cannot do without the vacuum cleaner … A vacuum cleaner cannot wait … There's always some thing." A more significant example would be Beth's situation which is enmeshed in contingent relations. Having quit school in Grade 9 because of family unrest and illness, Beth, now in her forties, is slowly upgrading her education, with the help of student loans. Finding welfare too humiliating, she is working part-time at a cut-rate clothing store. Not being able to afford to live alone, she is living with, and caring for, a demanding mother. She wants another part-time job but, never knowing her unpredictable work schedule until the week before, she has no consistent hours to offer another employer. One useful job would be delivering pizzas from 10 p.m. to 1 a.m., but she has neither license nor car. She has been saving money to take driving lessons, but much of her surplus goes to medication for some health problems. This is contingency with a vengeance, leaving scarcely a move to Beth that is her own and free.

Immobility and Isolation

Informants felt constrained by their relative immobility in a distanced and mobile society. The single mothers found themselves slowed to a child's pace. If there is a free concert in the park, they think, it is too much trouble to take the children and it will cost money. "And you shy away from it," Stephanie commented. "You get to the point where you don't do it. And you do become very isolated." (Add to that the feeling of not quite fitting into the pattern of couples and "double parents.") Children are expensive and troublesome to take on the bus, so families venture out less frequently. A single mother may limit her transportation to cab fare on the main monthly shopping trip. There was a strong desire for more affordable (i.e., subsidized) transportation for those on fixed incomes. People yearned for affordable bus passes which would unlock so many possibilities for them (even more so if day-care were also available). They would be able to do more varied and economical food shopping, be able to more easily search for jobs, be able to go to libraries and recreation centres, be able to visit relatives and friends, and be able to go to the gym or the doctor or the drop-in centre. Louise missed Holland, where "you are more independent, you can ride your bike … downtown, everything is close by." In Canada, by contrast, "everything is so big … There is not enough transportation."

Another single mother, Nancy, finds her immobility especially painful because it contrasts with her ex-husband's ease of move-ment. He takes the children to an annual picnic at Niagara Falls, and to Marineland and Canada's Wonderland — and she cannot.

> What with the bus fare and the train fare going up all the time, it's ridiculous, you know. Hey, I'd have to spend as much on the bus and train fare, plus being up there, as I would on two months' worth of groceries. It's just not worthwhile for me.

Keeping in mind Stephanie's earlier comments about wanting to be a strong example for her children, it would seem hard for women like Nancy — whose relative immobility is the result of the unequal economic situation after the break-up — to offer a dynamic exam-ple which would appeal to the young. Her children complain, "we never do anything."

To counter poverty's immobilization, informants make forays into a circumscribed social and neighbourhood circle. Stephanie values the co-op she lives in, which allows her to get out and around. Nancy values the four neighbours in her public housing complex who are within calling distance if her daughter ever needs assis-tance. People value the proximity of the doctor and their friends.

The most enthusiastic praiser of community is Robert, a single man with modest needs, who loves his east London neighbourhood.

> This is my stomping grounds. This is my area, out East — downtown I would be lost. If I need anything, my bank is just up the street, my Goodwill, my thrift shop. "I like shopping and I like the people." I have everything I need from Adelaide Street east on.

Of course, informants received money and support from their families, who occasionally sent "care packages" of nutritious food at various times.

Conclusion

The notion of freedom held out by the new right partisans of the market is a limiting one, indicating the absence of interference. But if we widen the notion to include "providing opportunity,"[84] then the market is a place of unfreedom for the poor. Theirs is the freedom to take jobs that subvert self-esteem and to receive wages that guarantee poverty; theirs is not the freedom to do, but to be done onto by employers and other winners in employed society. Freedom is not an abstract right when we are in an interdependent world, but is a situated product of a defining context. By virtue of our class society's segregation of the poor, its refusal to employ and pay people according to *their* needs not the needs of capital, and due to the bidding upward of the skill and educational requirements for decent-paying jobs, the poor are mired in an impoverishing class situation. Poverty is situated unfreedom. When Sandra was asked, "How is it for you being out of work? How does that feel?," her answer was bitter: "Like shit, like hell." Then Daniel broke in, "She said it for me." Then Sandra again: "You have to live with it." We must try to experience that bitter taste of unfreedom before we give in to the abstractions of freedom.

Absence of interference from government removes the means of granting opportunities for the poor to transcend the obstacles placed in their path by market society. New-right freedom, un-checked, entails the death of the practice of freedom by the poor, who will increasingly be controlled by Welfare officials and police.

---

[84] Taylor-Gooby, *Social Change*, 51.

Kevin had a critical moment in the destitute aftermath of his layoff. He had been living on popcorn and porridge. He stood there, his energy level low and adding to his depression, and thought, "I mean you're not getting ahead anywhere — so why bother trying, at anything?" What is this experience of social death but the implosive falling in on itself of a victim of the unrestrained practice of market freedom?

3

"A": Moralistic Giving of Charity

*T*he role configuration of moralistic giving of charity was found among service providers with a fundamentalist Christian or traditional Catholic cast, working in organizations like the London Food Bank and long-standing religious charities like the Christian Army[85] and those working out of Catholic parishes. This configuring mode presents the provider as clothed in moral righteousness and respectability, standing at the gate of societal goods (and of heaven, in a sense), showing both love and judgment to all who approach. The low-income person is altercast as a self-revealing dependent, who is seen, in biblical terms, as a sheep that has strayed from the conventional path of moral order. In the Foucauldian conceptual language introduced in Chapter 1, the provider's project here is anti-pauperism; i.e., socializing the social "bacteria" that might infect the moral order.

Why "moralistic"? The reader who peruses the short descriptions of the service providers in the Appendix will note the commonness of religious orientations and roles, and indeed moral concerns (more or less explicit) are found across the spectrum of configuring modes from "A" to "E." *This* configuring mode, though, is unique among the others as wanting to "moralize" the poor. To "moralize," as a transitive verb, is to "change the condition or aspect of (a person or thing) by moral talk or reflection; improve the morals of" (*Oxford English Dictionary*). Why do these providers wish to moralize low-income people? The reason seems to be that the poor are "in sin." Individual sin requires being put on the path towards individual salvation, hopefully, by the shepherding service provider. (As we move from "A" to "E," the definition of sin or moral turpitude widens out to "social sin;" e.g., by unjust tax policies, employer

---

[85] The names of organizations and individuals are made up.

practices and the like which are addressable by efforts for collective change or "redemption." The religious language is of course dropped, but not the moral nature of the critique.)

Three general practices in this mode work to configure low-income people who come for help. In the meanings and rituals of these practices are embedded expectations of exchange and asymmetrical power relations. The three are: individualizing and decontextualizing, maintaining paternalistic control, and ministering and moral guiding.

Individualizing and Decontextualizing

As we go from the "A" side of the spectrum to the "E", there is a shifting plane of typification: from an individualistic types-of-people construct to a more collectivist types-of-situation (or structure) one. Low-income persons are construed in their relations with "A" as a particular type of person — rather than, say, a complex amalgam of socio-economic, ethnocultural, psychological and familial circumstances. That there is thought to be a poor *type* is shown by the undifferentiated references to *"the poor"* in the interviews with these providers. This archetypal poor person is seen as, essentially, spiritually and humanly flawed. Out of the struggles of this defective person is heard a summons or mandate for the service provider: to correct, to discipline, and to help the person overcome his or her shortcomings. The service provider individualizes poverty, abstracting it from the situational or group contexts of low-income people, and sets it into a new moralized context which is charged with meaning for the provider. An example of the individualistic tone is the description by Harold, an official at the London City Food Bank, where he depicts individuals inserted non-interactively into their contexts: "What we're trying to do in the end is leaving a person standing alone with his community and feeling comfortable. Leaving a person standing alone with his family and feeling comfortable. Leaving a person standing alone with his God and feeling comfortable. These things put together make up for dignity."

What are the imputed characteristics of "The Poor"? What is "the Plight of the Needy" (to inflect their own words), according to these providers? Firstly, the poor are *children* who have lost their innocence. Harold finds the poor to be "terrible realists. They lost their ideals years ago." What brought about this corruption of the innocents? It was Welfare programs. We providers, says he, must deal with this "lethargy we have placed upon the poor by [our] doing all the blinking work for them." When the interviewer asked why not take away social services, he answered, "You can't do that any more than you can do that to a child."

The "shepherd" here is seeking out his "sheep," but they are scattered and intractable. What is the innocence Harold pines for but the docile humanity that is *his* project to redeem? ["Infantilization of the poor," Procacci writes, "and valorization of childhood as a vehicle for socialization: the two operations go together as technical supports for an immense enterprise of permanent educability."[86]] But Harold is upset at the difficulty of engaging the poor in the religious education he has in mind for them. Perhaps thinking of the large numbers in the food bank, he laments how service providers treat the poor "as sort of mindless people," just giving them what they want, whether food baskets, furniture, or clothes. What they need is individual, not impersonal, care. Why are they not getting it?

> [I]n the vast majority I sense nothing but apathy, lethargy, and ambivalence. We're just like a store to these people; they don't have to pay ... [T]hey're not looking forward to a mental, social, or spiritual transaction. They're coming here for goods. And we've got to re-instruct them.

The poor are blamed for failing to commit to the "mental, social, or spiritual transaction" which will give *Harold's* life meaning. Little thought is given to the pressures that drive people to use food banks or to the psychic cost (and possible ineffectiveness) of their entering into a moralized personal transaction. The service provider feels thwarted by his inability to bring his construct, the poor person, into his own moralized domain.

The catalogue of disrespect goes on: the poor are untrustworthy, unmotivated, corrupted with self-interest. For Duncan, a director of a religious charity, the cause of poverty is the poor's inability to manage their money (though he admits welfare payments are low).

---

[86] Procacci, "Social economy," 165-166.

The market system, he thinks, is the land of plenty, such that, if you have a dream, the jobs are out there to fulfill it. The problem is with the individual who docs not strive or grasp for the ripe berries. For Duncan, the symbolic antipode to the ripe berries ready for plucking is *beer-drinking*. On his home visits, he looks for beer: "You can always see beer in the fridge or a case of beer on the floor ... It's really bad to get into the drinking." He is interpreting beer-drinking in one way only, as emblematic of the downward forces in the flawed character of the poor.

The poor are thought to be lazy, and this is a very important part of the public stereotype of low-income people. Continuing his assault on the moral character of his construct of the poor person, Harold commented: "they'll sit there and wallow in their pile." "They have become lazy in looking for jobs; they have become lazy in really picking up their bootstraps and helping themselves to do it." Duncan thinks that 90 percent of them do not want to better their situation. He sees them when the welfare runs out and they are reduced to indigence. Noticing the children running around, he comments condescendingly: "You have pity on them because they'll never know anything else." They are in a welfare rut and only want to exist at the most basic level.

What is the source of this torpor and laziness? Part of it is interpreted as unredeemed human nature, it being thought that people will naturally sink into sin without the disciplining and vigilant ministrations of their superiors. Another part is external. Laziness, according to Harold, is "a disease they have acquired ... that's been given to them by a government and by social agencies that put them in this rut in the first place." The language of infection hints at the real enemy coming into view: pauperism. These people are not committed to the societal project of sacrificing their gratifications to become workers and consumers. And who has fed these parasites? The social agencies, whose many goods given to the poor have sapped the poor's self-disciplined productivity. The solution, thinks Harold, is to coordinate the social agencies so that the poor do not become corrupted by getting more than they deserve. For "coordination," read "power" — i.e., organizational power in the social services field in its war against pauperism.

Though these service providers' primary mode is moralistic giving, other configuring strains were discernible. Duncan thinks that corporations should be taxed more to help the poor. A few of them commented on the disincentives to find employment that are built into the Welfare system. Kenneth (of the Christian Army) approved the construction of private rooms for some of the men at the mission, as opposed to the older dormitories. He defends the men who stay at the mission, differentiating them from those lower down the scale — the sleepers and drunks under the bridge. (This discriminatory assessment tends to fit into the anti-pauperism thesis, though, in that he is critical of those who are not amenable to the project of control.)

To conclude this practice, the abstracting from real-world contexts in role configuration "A" is abetted by its own isolation from those very contexts outside its jurisdiction. The service providers here deal with low-income people in predictable, even ritual, postures of need at desperate times — queuing, receiving food, looking down and so forth. When their stringent rules or moralistic expectancies are violated, their untrusting prophecies about the poor are fulfilled. They are not involved with low-income people outside the service provider's domain — in their communities, or political struggles, or family life — nor are they at home in or informed about the wider urban or political arenas. The service provider is trying to carve out a moralized niche or context away from the world where its own particular giving — with its strong self-validating element — can be offered and received.

Configuration "A" views the members of the lower class "as the authors of their fate"[87] or at least co-authors with the agencies and government — so that there is a victim-blaming element. Underlying the religious rhetoric is a profound contempt for the poor; indeed theirs is part of a wider public disrespect that is one of the defining features of poverty. Underlying the contempt is a disdain for people who are different, who are not yoked into the dominant productivist and consumer orientations which are accorded (implicit) moral primacy. Also there is frustration at the lack of fulfillment of a *calling*, both of individual providers and of an incipient moral community. This moralistic mission will now be analyzed as a practice in its own right.

---

[87] Miller, "Poverty and respect," 226.

Ministering and Moral Guiding

The decontextualizing of poverty in configuration "A" is remarkable; the world is transformed as if by magic. No mention is made of the declining real value of the minimum wage, the increase in part-time and low-wage jobs, or any empirical constraint on the condition of low-income people. A spiritual overlay is placed on top of the usual view of society. Poor people and their circumstances, as well as service providers, are set into an allegorical narrative, whose themes are sin, weakness, redemption, and personal defeat and triumph. This repainting of the picture of society is part of the moral right's effort to move into the vacuum left by the ebbing away of governmental programs. A good statement of this revisioning of reality and policy is given by Ralph Harris:

> [W]e must work towards a system that, first, confines "free" resources to deserving victims of adversity; and, second, accompanies cash with counselling and pastoral care which ministers to each individual's disability or deficiency. Since care is best lavished by those with love for their handicapped neighbour, it is better provided wherever possible in the local community and by voluntary action which, like mercy, blesses giver and receiver.[88]

This Christian mandate is endorsed by Harold — though he thinks it is beyond practical implementation at the Food Bank — who wants Church ideas and involvement to permeate the care for the disadvantaged. What the Christian mandate means to Harold is "caring for the human soul, about loving children, helping them come to that openness and understanding."

The classic expression of the hoped-for linkage between material helping and spiritual guidance is the Christian Army's slogan of "soup and salvation." "Soup," nourishing the physical and material needs of the poor, draws them in so that the troops can do the real work of the organization, "salvation" (through preaching, singing and counselling). There are a few assumptions at work here. One is that destitution is a constant and will provide a steady supply of souls to keep the workers busy. Another assumption is that poor people need saving, that they are cast down morally and need lifting

---

[88] Quoted in Hewitt, *Welfare, Ideology and Need*, 101. The quote is from Harris, *Beyond the Welfare*, 26.

up. The equation of destitution with lack of salvation (or moral degradation) has limited objective validity outside of the self-reinforcing role configuration imposed by the organization — which connects the fulfillment of giver and receiver. To define others as in need of salvation is the start of the reciprocal process of saving self and organization. You need the poor *to be saved* (in both senses, self and other).

Jacob, an official with a men's mission whose configuring modes were twofold (moralistic and needs responding), wants to be an exemplar for the poor. He wants the trajectory of his life (from sleeping under bridges all the way up to respected leadership in the social services community) to be the model for the poor individual's struggle upward in the present-day mission. His reflections on the role of service provider are revelatory:

> The poor ... do get an awful lot of good people working with them. They draw some of the best people in the world ... Maybe we're helping ourselves ... That's where we get our kicks somehow. There's hardly anyone in this line of work that doesn't have some tremendous need of their own ... [Y]ou just manage to work it out through helping the other fellow as well as helping yourself too.

The provider and recipient are locked in a grip of mutual need.

Service providers with this role configuration are looking for faults in their dependent "clients," as well as ways to improve their habits and moral character. This mode of providing has a long lineage in Canada. One of the country's first public welfare guardians, J. J. Kelso, found it in orphanages in the late 19th century. Orphanage children were, in his words, "moved about all day like pieces of machinery and their education consisted chiefly of scolding, fault-finding, and lectures on behaviour, humility and respect for the good ladies who were doing so much for them."[89] We must, the "fault-finding" mindset maintains, guard against their beer-drinking, their unwise spending of money and their lax parenting practices. Kenneth describes with almost voluptuous pleasure his research and discovery of welfare clients back in the Maritimes who lied and cheated the system. In one case, the

---

[89] Quoted in Rooke and Schnell, "Guttersnipes," 93.

husband had been working in Hamilton and helping the family out. Kenneth had discovered this, and when his wife came to him for a Christmas basket, he refused her. "Oh boy, these people are lying through their teeth. And the only reason I ever refused a person was if they ever lied to me and I caught them." The vigilance at identifying sin was only the negative side of a moral improvement project which these providers were embarked on. Kenneth insisted that he and his fellow providers were here to serve, not to help themselves. They want to be "able to see the person improve."

Resentment of Those Who Resist Moral Improvement

These interviews bristle with a pent-up moral influence in search of a subject it can breathe life into. Kenneth concedes that the poor are not the best people, but we have to recognize them as people "and do what we can to make their life better, to improve their lifestyle." To those he suspected of taking advantage of free food, he invited them to "sit down with me and go over your budget with me" so that they would arrive jointly at a dollar figure for food money (say, $60 a month). He has asked the poor: "'Are you willing to give me that $60 a month and I'll feed you three meals a day for the whole month? And I haven't had one taker." That he has had no takers is proof, for him, of the refractory nature of the poor. That it has not occurred to him that his proposal is controlling, humiliating and impractical is proof, for the social analyst, that Kenneth's empathy is unengaged — for he is relating to a construct of a poor person, not the real thing.

The chilling coexistence of Christian "virtues" with an overmastering resentment is starkly expressed in Harold's interview. He wants the poor at the Food Bank to stop focusing on the goods, and know that "when they come here, they're with people who really like them and ... [they should] sit down and have coffee with us and ... explain their problems." He wants a "synthesis" with them. But all they are interested in is the food, which enrages Harold:

> But when they come here [to the food bank], ... they're not thinking of the good the Church does, or the gospel of Jesus Christ. They're not thinking of social agencies and the fact that they've been around for 20 or 30 years and they're wonderful and they're our main suppliers. They're not thinking of us at all.

With the free food, all sorts of people are "seen to be coming out of the woodwork" now. "There is a trend towards more and more help, and if they can get it free, they're going to get it free." What does "free" mean here? It means getting food without "paying" Harold what he needs. When the implicit expectations that the poor person must stay, listen, take instruction, etc., are violated, the official feels cheated, used, and cynical. With the poor failing to validate the service provider's role by presenting stories and a pliable nature, the transaction between helper and helped — from the needful helper's standpoint — is unconsummated and unsynthesized. Faced with this "materialism" and spiritual recalcitrance, Harold counsels forgiveness. "You hurt me when you said that, even when I was trying to help you as a needy person. I'll let that roll off my back because Christ has taught me that I've done the same things to him and he has forgiven." Harold is picking up all signals from low-income people with a particular kind of fundamentalist, Biblical receiver. It is not that such a theological perspective necessitates such a lack of empathy (for some of the attentive helpers in role "C" are fundamentalist), but it is used by Harold to express his overweening emotional investment in the helping vocation, with its mixture of pious condescension and resentment towards poor people.

The Social Community

When Kenneth worked in the Christian Army in Moncton, New Brunswick, all the charity and social service workers knew each other as well as most of the recipients. Coming out of that smaller, ethnically homogeneous and culturally traditional context, Kenneth cherishes that simpler *gemeinschaft* model where people knew their roles and their place. He is nostalgic for a cohesive, well-controlled community where he and others can minister to the poor within the charity framework. But the larger, impersonal urban situation he finds himself in — with its greater diversity of people and organization, its claims to individual rights, its variety of sources of provision — makes it difficult for people like him to see that they are improving the lives of the poor.

This notion of a "social community" — with its distinct ideological slant to the moral right — is expressed most clearly by Harold. He wants a humble Christian community of the wounded and their healers. The churches would be important to infuse the community with proper themes and values. Christian business figures and companies would supply resources and teachers. "We work extensively with business and find them to be most open to us. Corporate business can help us get out of the malaise we're in."

Turning to the government, Harold insists that there is no money and, anyway, "the bureaucratic system can't create." The social community will need to rely on volunteers: "The volunteer way is going to be the only way of the future." But no one wants to confront that, because we are psychologically wedded to the notion that it's "mainly government's responsibility to take care of the poor in the community." In Harold's view, "it is the *community's* responsibility to take care of the poor, not the government or tax dollars."

Under cover of a meek Christian community is a politicized, counter-ideological alternative to the welfare state. It will tolerate no rivals to its own configuring power over the disadvantaged.

We need to downplay the current emphasis on rights. In Harold's words: "Society turns to the Bill [sic] of Rights, to the constitution. Christians don't need that; they have the Bible." Likewise, the providers in "A" criticize the idea of a guaranteed annual income (GAI). The GAI entitles people to "free" money — that is, money not tied to the control and discretionary strategies of career providers like Duncan and Harold. The GAI is "not going to make people productive. The only way people get productive is *when one personality draws along next to another* and not when somebody goes to a mailbox and gets a government cheque" (emphasis added). This is the anti-pauperism project clearly revealed: moralistic, personalistic socialization of the poor into a monolithic and normative image of *homo economicus.*

The moral right opposes universalistic welfare measures and entitlements, favouring instead increased selectivity in the application of welfare. In power terms, the *moral right* that wants to do the selecting and the administering. Against the forces of secularization, of rights, of urban diversity, of bureaucratic complexities, they want to reinstate the moral gate-keeping functions of a moralistic elite presiding over a simpler, more homogeneous time. The control aspects of this project constitutes our third practice.

Maintaining Paternalistic Control

Political subjectification works, according to Mitchell Dean, "by the establishment of forms of self-relation through disciplinary practices and techniques of surveillance, and through the material organization of conduct in time-space."[90] This gives us a way of organizing the control strategies of the "A" providers: firstly, the micro strategies of discipline and surveillance and, secondly, the effort to achieve community-wide controls over spacing and timing.

Disciplinary Practices and Techniques of Surveillance

There are many poor people who stay away from the social services field altogether. They do not file for welfare, do not show up at the food outlets, hostels, soup kitchens, or drop-in centres. Such people live with family members or friends, or hole up in squatter flats in condemned buildings. To make any sort of contact with the charities of the social service field, you must submit to a system that will process your identity (the exception is the Soup Kitchen). If you do not show I.D. to the Christian Army, you are sent to the police station to be identified and cleared before you can return and receive your food or lodgings. In places whose accommodations are funded by a per diem contribution from city welfare, you must fill out an application form from Welfare. A well-known religious charity and the food bank require, between them, the birth certificate, social insurance number, proof of address, name of social worker, and welfare stub. Those in line for Christmas baskets must have the relevant papers in hand or they are sent away. To receive food at the Food Bank, you must submit to detailed processing. (Although the low-income informants in the study did not single out the Food Bank for negative comment, one community activist, Joseph, reported that the poor people in his union complained that the Food Bank personnel made you feel that it was their own food they were giving out.)

The service providers in configuration "A," as was mentioned earlier, tend to be unhappy or resigned about giving out food without personal contact. Duncan particularly fought the establishment of a food bank in a nearby church because it was "against

---

[90] Dean, "'A social structure'," 157.

our principle. We want to be able to go to the individuals who need the help and find out what the circumstances are so that we can help them, instead of just saying, 'come down to the food bank and get a bag of groceries'."

What is the nature of the personal contact Duncan wishes to have with the families who are out of food and money near the end of the month? Unlike the Welfare interview which is filled with questions about assets, expenses and needs, the questions from the charity-givers are more intimate and invasive about applicants' private identities and stories.

> We visit them and we sit down with them and say, "Well, what's the problem? What do you need?" Then they tell us the story and, if we believe it, we'll say, "Well, when will you be getting help?"

Duncan wants to be convinced of the coherence and credibility of the applicant's need. Is this family deserving of the scarce resources of goods and esteem which he feels deputized to protect? The look around the place, and mode of listening to private facts, suggest the uniform manner of an inspector of morals.

Listening to the narratives of the poor is a form of work for the provider that lies at the heart of their transaction. They suffer through the sad stories: checking for inconsistencies, sifting for possibilities for help and listening for moral lessons. (Underlining the value of these stories, Harold believes that the poor could make a large impact on society by telling them, eloquently, to corporations and the media.) On a more analytical level, what is the nature of the transaction here? The poor obtain basic goods which they cannot afford on the private market. On the other side, the non-poor learn of the passage of degraded humanity and, of course, remind themselves of their own compassion and usefulness. Most importantly, the stories carry the exceptionalistic message that poverty is about people hitting bottom, rather than the universalistic one that poverty is about processes maintained by the non-poor which force people down.

If he and his fellow worker believe the story, the family gets a voucher. (When he became director of his parish-based charity, Duncan immediately replaced the giving of cash to the recipients with a voucher system.) With voucher in hand, the recipients "have to show the manager their ID and he/she generally checks their order. The cashiers are very good; they all know our vouchers and they know the rules now." When a poor recipient is out of gas, the "helping" is even more humiliating (perhaps stemming from Duncan's lack of acceptance of poor people who own cars). "We take them over to the gas station and pay for it ourself, *out of our own pocket*, and then get a receipt" (emphasis added). Mistrustful of poor people who might spend money on alcohol, he has created a system of infantilizing the poor, making them (regardless of circumstances) into shame-faced children.

Disrespect is not just attitudinal any more but built into the rituals and routines of Duncan's organization. The material resources it controls are small but strategically important to the poor in the parishes. At a time when poverty has brought his clients to their knees, Duncan makes them crawl. The transaction is an identity set-up; it seems dialogic, but is decidedly one-sided and a cheat. The poor must exchange their personal identities and stories for goods on the public system. They get things they need, but there is a personal rejection of their identity by the provider. The service provider says, "Share with me your problems, bare your soul," and then drops them to the floor with pity and disapproval.[91]

The rigour of the gate-keeping and the stinginess of the support may be partly attributable to the feeling by some providers that the social wage and benefits on welfare are not bad. Along with the free benefits, $1000 a month tax-free for a person living with two or three children in low-rental apartments looks to Duncan like a reasonable wage and a possible disincentive to get off of welfare. Indeed he thinks that if you make welfare too generous workers will quit their jobs to get on it. His remarks require class analysis. Workers in the religious agencies have (self-admittedly) low salaries. This might increase the zeal with which they regulate the flow of surplus social wages to the "less deserving" poor. Their market incomes giving little return on effort, these providers will be exacting on those who claim compensation for less effort than their own.

Duncan asks the poor if they need spiritual help. "Most of the time they don't want us even to speak about spirituality, because

---

[91] This is an insight of Morgan Gardner's.

they're not in the proper mood. They're starving to death so they don't want to talk religion." But why would a poor person buy into a religious perspective that constructs their poverty as "sin" and the demeaning help they receive as "charity" and "love"? You might be "saved" in a spiritual sense, but your identity would be negated. It would be a more interesting sociological problem if they *agreed* with the construction placed on their poverty by this kind of religion. Indeed, the lack of receptivity to these religious messages may be construed as a form of *resistance*. It is admittedly a passive mode, but that is one of the only methods open to children, real or putative. It may be the way of preserving self-respect and mental space for interpretations that go beyond the ones configured for them by the providers.

Coordination and Control at the Community Level

In Moncton, Kenneth had worked up a master list of all those that required help at Christmas and was about to do the same thing year round. Different organizations could then cover different groupings of recipients and they could ensure that people did not abuse the system. But in London, it is a less tightly managed system and more of a free market. There are too many outlets for the providers' liking and too many rights and unsupervised freedoms. A man can work the system and spend the money that he saves on food on alcohol and other vices. Ex-psychiatric patients' rights to refuse institutionalization "handcuff" the Christian Army's attempt to hospitalize the unruly mentally ill in the community.

As a counter-strategy to the loss of monopoly control that these organizations used to enjoy, there is a movement to coordinate activities and monitor client usage by placing everyone on the computer. "We're on a computerized system now," says Duncan. "The city puts it on computer so that we know exactly what they're getting." This is especially useful for Christmas baskets; at Christmas, Duncan finds, a lot of poor people get pretty "hoggish," wanting four or five baskets. Harold wants the food to be monitored, not only to avoid abuse, but to condition the poor to expect less and less. Offended by the fact that the poor can get $300 worth of food in a month when they do not need it, Harold wants a coordinated cutback of their receipt of food to once a month from a different agency — "so that we are cutting back these people but never to the point of despair." He wants them weaned off the system, "to get them to move out on their own, to remove some of the disincentives ... that have kept them in the social system in the way that it is." These service providers want a managed system with powers given to its administrators — the power to maintain an artificial scarcity of goods, and the discretionary power over who gets resources and who does not, and what must be done to get them.

Concluding Analysis

The enemy of this role configuration is pauperism, not poverty or inequality, the latter being taken as a natural fact of life in industrial society. The poor who were most appreciated were those who renounced pauperism; i.e., renounced their insubordination, independence, wilfulness and resistance to duty. They took the hand of the helper and walked the path to disciplined, gratification-deferring normalcy. What is absent in the interviews is any sense of poor individuals as being *adults*, fellow citizens, interlocutors in their own life conditions. How unknowledgeable these service providers seem about the actual, situated men and women behind the religious stereotypes. How unreflective they were about the dovetailing of their own self-construction with the other-construction of the self-revealing dependants they dealt with each day (who were trying to keep their distance). When looking in vain for detailed social knowledge beyond the cardboard cut-out of "the poor," we might consider Procacci's reminder that, for such a project as this, "pauperism is a pretext."

> The homogeneous consistency of the category of pauperism, used without any concern to break it down into a distinct conception of the various micropopulations it brackets together, indicates its fictitious character: what is really designated by the term is ... the ensemble of adversities/adversaries which confront the project of social order.[92]

The homunculus "poor person" was, on the surface, the site of warring forces of spiritual decay and redemptive potential in a biblically resonant narrative. But decoding the narrative shows us

---

[92] Procacci, "Social economy," 163.

service providers who are embarked on the constitution of a
different subject than the productive subject. The poor here are the
site of a project of normalization devoted to shaping them into
docile subjects of a variety of control strategies. Entitlement is
extinguished, government interventions rolled back, and what is
left, alone and defenceless, is the poor and grateful subject of the
self-justifying moral uplift of a conservative elite.

But there was also a class subtext under the religious rhetoric —
it was the working poor who were placed as gate-keepers of
societal transfers which were sought by their "competitors," the
subsidized poor (suspected of being undeserving). This may be an
ingredient of the rancour of the givers. But even more damaging
than rancour is the withholding of *respect*, which is one of the main
deprivations of the help offered here. If we view a group as deficient
in humanity, it makes it easier for us to mistreat them without a
sense of guilt. "We" can then treat "them" like a caste. The lack of
free unrestrained dialogue and the lack of solidarity across the
divide between provider and recipient is striking. Synergistic ties
are almost wholly lacking in the encounter, as we draw on their
weakness as the source of our strength. The differences and defects
one observes in the destitute that stand before us bolster our own
sense of being in control, well-connected and personally powerful.
The language of charity and ideals masks, even to the providers'
selves, a project of domination.

Nietzsche's conception that values — whether fundamentalist
Christian, liberal-humanist, or whatever — are expressions of the
will to power, and that morality is rooted in resentment, may be
relevant to role configuration "A" (among others). We do not have
to accept his skewed depiction of one form of Christianity as being
representative of the whole, to apply his insights to our moralizing
givers. "[F]aith moves no mountains but *puts* mountains where there
are none … Christianity *needs* sickness … [T]o *make* sick is the true,
secret purpose of the whole system of redemptive procedures
constructed by the church."[93]

---

[93] Nietzsche, "The antichrist," 632.

The last word will be given to a few of our low-income informants (whose fuller reactions will be presented in Chapter 8 on receiving and acting). One woman refused to go to a particular parish agency or a women's mission because "It's too degrading. They question you as to why you can't afford to buy food. And you're going, 'Hey, look at my bills'."

A single disabled man, Mark, resented the required presentation of self before appraising charity-givers. "Once charity is given, there is almost an obligation ... The person who is giving the charity has the power to say whether or not this person is worthy of it." He balked at the moral pressure to conform which was built into the encounter. People who receive charity have to act in a certain way that society deems appropriate. But he affirmed that the poor should have the benefits of living as their right, not because they meet the selective discretionary criteria of social judges. The rights should not be contingent on what you do for the country or if you are a good or bad person, but just "a matter of their existence," i.e., the simple fact of one's needs.

4

"B": Bureaucratic Subsidizing

*T*he role configuration, "bureaucratic subsidizing," was drawn from interviews with officials and workers in the "local state" — chiefly, the Canada Employment Centre, city welfare, and, to a lesser extent, Neighbourhood Legal Aid. The local state is nested within larger political jurisdictions, whose legislative and policy guidelines it must follow. The Canada Employment Centre enacts procedures and directives which emanate from the Employment and Immigration bureaucracy in Ottawa, as well as the Unemployment Insurance Act. City Welfare follows guidelines from the provincial and municipal governments and applies the provisions of the General Welfare Assistance Act. Welfare is also accountable to city politicians, who must answer to ratepayers/voters for the money they spend.

The recipient is construed as a "self-revealing client with legal-bureaucratic rights." The difference from the organizations discussed in the previous chapter is that the social service bureaucracies have clients with very real legal entitlements (e.g., last month's rent, incomes-in-kind, shelter allowance), which limit the organization's discretionary treatment of them. By contrast, in the charity organizations the extent and kinds of discretion can vary according to their mandate and the service-workers' perception of that mandate.

Across the counter or phone line is the official. We have represented the self-presentation as "bureaucratic subsidizing" not because that is *all* the official does, but that, in most cases, the official's mandate is to defend public monies: to withhold them from the legally disentitled and to dispense them (within a framework of rules) to the entitled. So "helping the poor" may be an individual motive of the service provider but, *qua* official, the task (reduced to its essentials) is to administer and discern eligibility for the public transfers controlled by the state. Not surprisingly, there is a sense conveyed by the interviewed official of a partitioning of self and voice. While sitting in the official's chair and office, the person feels that the System must speak through her. Suzette, an official at Unemployment Insurance, often distinguished her own personal view from the official one she represents during contacts with the public. She professed interest in the present study personally but did not think the bureaucracy would want it. She evaded questions of a political, non-official kind by saying that if she were having coffee with the interviewer she could offer an opinion. Others gave unattributable personal answers, anxious to distinguish their personal and official voices.

Conceptual Introduction

Because the state domain is so central to the social services/action field and so important as a mediating link between people and the market, we present some guiding concepts. There is a distinction made by Habermas between the purposive rationality of the formal bureaucracy and the communicative rationality of the lifeworld — which he applies to the welfare state. Redistribution in the welfare state permits a sharing of surplus value that helps meet the real-world needs of non-market participants and helps ensure their citizenship. But the provision of this support is highly abstract. "For in reality, benefits are fixed in relation to prevailing levels of monetary and exchange value and so drawn into the abstract commodity form."[94] People's entitlements are rarely universal but are formally set out in selective, rule-bound, and usually means-tested requirements. A vast bureaucracy is established to ascertain eligibility, then to continue to monitor it in the light of changing wage, marital, or other situational factors. What becomes lost in this instrumentally rational system, according to Habermas, is the communicative rationality of living persons sharing a lifeworld.[95] Applied to our topic of relations between low-income people and service providers, this shared lived experience would entail an unrestrained cultural dialogue among people on the interpretations of their needs and dependencies, as well as their desires to give and develop.

---

[94] Hewitt, *Welfare, Ideology and Need*, 107.

[95] Habermas, "Historical materialism."

The "JAT" (Fraser)

For a more precise account of how the welfare system changes
and processes people's life problems and needs (often quite
political) into administrable needs, we turn to Fraser's charac-
terization of the (U.S.) welfare system as a "juridical-administrative-
therapeutic state apparatus" (JAT).[96] The *juridical* element of the
JAT situates recipients in relation to the legal system by the denial
or granting of rights to benefits. There seems to be something of a
gender divide juridically. In what Fraser calls the more "masculine"
subsystem of, say, social insurance, clients are entitled to benefits
and have legal protection against arbitrary withholding; while in
the more "feminine" subsystem of social assistance, rights are either
weak or lacking, and more discretion is exercised to control clients.

In the *administrative* element, subjects must act like petitioners
to a bureaucracy that has the power to decide whether their claim
meets the proper criteria. In the "masculine" subsystem, subjects
need to show that they meet the system's criteria of entitlement;
while in the "feminine" subsystem, subjects must show that they
meet the system's criteria of needfulness. Women tend to be
constructed as dependent clients, often receiving predefined services; while men (according to Fraser) are more likely to be
constructed as consumers, receiving cash.

In the third element of the JAT, the *therapeutic*, attention is given
to "mental health" and "character" problems or, less paternalisti-
cally, to lifestyle dysfunctions — which call for counselling, tutoring
and group therapy sessions. The assumption here is that if, say,
young women come to know their deep emotional problems, they
will not have unwanted pregnancies. Fraser observes "the tendency
of especially 'feminine' social-welfare programs to construct gen-
der-political and political-economic problems as individual, psychological problems."[97]

In all cases, the experienced and interpreted needs of people are
recast into administratively defined needs and, since "the latter are
not necessarily isomorphic to the former, the possibility of a gap

[96] Fraser, "Women, Welfare," 154 ff.

[97] Ibid., 155.

between them arises."[98] This notion of a *gap* is crucial. Firstly, it offers a cogent mandate and *raison d'être* for interpretive-critical social research and analysis which will look for and thematize this gap. Secondly, it will alert us to the possibility that Fraser points to, that women's frequent treatment as stigmatized deviants in the welfare system has increased this gap. And, finally, we may start to notice instances (especially in the therapeutic corners of the field) where people's lived experience is made to fit the administrative version of their need, and not the reverse.

Capillary Power (Foucault)

Foucault thought that social policy was a mechanism of the state for making use of and channelling power through all parts of the society. Power did not simply descend from a leader or elite but ascended from freely constructed subjects which had internalized means of self-discipline. Subjects were constituted by power; their bodily traces, modes of discourse, self-conceptions, improvement regimes and so on, were vectors of force relations impinging at this and at other levels of the social body. In Hewitt's words:

> Power is exercised upon, through and by the subject. For example, social policy constructs subjects upon whom power is inscribed (e.g., deprived individuals and neighbourhoods); it provides a capillary through which state power is circulated throughout the social body (administrative apparatuses affecting family life); and, by its own power, social policy establishes and preserves its interests (by legitimating governmental, professional, academic and research practices).[99]

The force relation, not equal but dynamic and dialogic, connects caseworker and client, men and women, individual and group in "strategies of power ranging from constructive complicity to outright repression."[100]

---

[98] Ibid.

[99] Hewitt, *Welfare, Ideology and Need*, 159.

[100] Ibid., 159-160.

Pastoral and Citizenship Aspects of the State

Keeping in mind that power is not simply repressive, silencing, externally directive — but may be liberative, discursive and internally guiding the projects of acting subjects — we can then see the state as a dual (and somewhat contradictory) project of political subjectification, having both pastoral and citizenship aspects. The state constructs subjects as clients to be administered and socialized to serve governmental purposes (pastoral), but can also construct subjects as responsible, independent members of a *polis* (citizenship).

The political approach does not leave it up to individual citizens to unintentionally "happen on" the good society in the course of their selfish daily pursuits but aims to provide an authoritative, legitimate instrument which can direct potentially chaotic action to serve the interests of all. The welfare state embodies a conception of the state as a moral agent. It is assumed that individuals and markets have interests, but the state's actions are potentially based on *dis*interest[101] — in the sense of impartial justice and absence of discrimination. Though the state may be bureaucratic, it alone can confer the entitlement to citizenship and be the guarantor of universal social rights based on norms of social justice. Its laws and policies and practices can protect equality and defend against the stratifying effects of the market. State laws are in part the sedimentation of the struggles of the marginalized for dignity and just participation in Canadian life.

Having conceptualized some of the elements of state power and potential, we now introduce the practices. The chief configurative practices in the state welfare domain are three: assessing and monitoring eligibility, abstracting from real-life situations into bureaucratic categories, and wielding discretion. Within these practices, what is being exchanged? How is power manifested? What empowering possibilities are held out to the low-income person, beyond the formulaic shape of the imposed social role?

---

[101] Wolfe, *Whose Keeper?*, 107.

Assessing and Monitoring Eligibility

To assess and monitor eligibility is the most important function of the city Welfare department. Members of the public and the politicians want Welfare to perform a kind of moral quality control with regard to the claimants to whom it transfers funds. When one of our service providers was asked about the Guaranteed Annual Income, her answer spoke volumes about the public accountability directed to Welfare:

> I think it would be great, but it will be a long time coming ... There is tremendous pressure in the community around all of these people on Welfare that are spending their money on ... beer and all those things that everybody thinks they shouldn't spend it on. And those people call their alderman and they call their politicians ... [A]ll kinds of complaints from people in the community calling ... and saying, "Do you know so and so is doing this? Do you know that so and so is doing that?" And as long as that pressure is there, I think that there is pressure for governments to feel that they are doing something to be accountable for the dollars that are being spent — hence the needs testing kind of thing that we go through.

She disagrees with the public perceptions, but think that they are a product of our ingrained values. "Our society blames people who don't work for their own situations," she added.

The accountability chain she describes — from welfare department to municipal politicians to ratepayer/voters — has been criticized by welfare state defenders. They want to source Welfare revenues from the province, not from the municipal property tax base. Ratepayers in the suburbs are disinclined to show solidarity with the poor when their rising property values yield higher taxes which help pay for welfare expenditures.

Being Processed for Eligibility

The present caseload in the London Welfare department is 260 clients per worker, which is among the highest levels in the province. Because of this staff overload, caseworkers are "providing more of an eligibility assessment monitoring than anything else," Margaret indicated. "It really works against a lot of sensitivity happening in the system that could be there." What is lost is the in-depth intervention, which includes counselling, continuous support and follow-up. She regrets that emotionally disturbed people who are deinstitutionalized do not have counsellors to provide them with a careful referral that would link them meaningfully to an agency that would help them. She continues: "Like there's a referral and a referral. The kind of referral our staff is often able to make is just simply to tell people about things, where they are, and how to go about it ... You have to be blind to not see that they need a lot more than financial assistance."

In its primary function of judging eligibility, Welfare is anything but superficial or cursory. The initial phone call requesting assistance is often crisis-driven and fraught with emotion. The clerical staff are admonished to be receptive and tactful with the caller, so as not to prepare a hostile recipient for the caseworker's initial home visit. In the first interview, the caseworker tries to encode the applicant's self-presentation into bureaucratic categories of need, upon which the binary assessment of eligible/ineligible will be based. The most common category of need that is excluded is a person who is working full-time; even if the income was a poverty wage, such a person is categorically ineligible. (If a couple applies for social assistance and the head of the family is working at a very low wage, Welfare can designate the other partner as "head of the family" who would then be categorically eligible. But that advantage would not, of course, apply to single parents.) If you are planning full-time schooling, you are ineligible for Unemployment Insurance — because everyone on UI is required to be actively looking for work and able to immediately accept it.

The application form in the first welfare interview is six pages long, covering highly personal information. No other eligibility assessment procedure is as intrusive as Welfare's needs-and-means tests. Relationships are plumbed as potential sources of income support; intimate questions about past history and present plans are asked; all assets both fixed and liquid are assessed as to whether they are exempt or non-exempt from the resources calculation (which is subtracted from the estimation of need). The caseworker is unmistakably the dominant interactant in a "power relationship," according to Margaret. "The caseworker walks into the room and what the client sees is: 'There's [the person who will decide] whether or not I get my rent paid, or food for next week.' There's a lot of power, and it makes it difficult to establish a good rapport." The monitoring is ongoing, with interviews occurring about once a month for employables and once every few months for unemployables. Despite the heavy caseload, and the lack of evidence of widespread welfare fraud, London's City Council has hired "welfare police" to increase fraud investigations and to make surprise home visits.

The reaction of the client to this intrusive personal and institutional power is fear and humiliation. One of our low-income informants, Julia, a pensioner from Toronto, had stayed in London while her husband was in hospital. He died and she had insufficient income to move back. She was forced to apply for public housing in London because it had rent geared to income. Each year Julia is questioned about her income, savings and many other personal details to ascertain what her subsidized rent will be in the following year. She found this very nasty and almost moved out; for her the administered life is "frightening." She contrasts this feeling of being boxed into subsidized housing with her situation in the St. Lawrence area of Toronto, where "nobody is aware that your rent is subsidized." It is as though the punishing Welfare procedures were deliberately calculated to reduce the number of clients by making it difficult to become and stay eligible.[102]

Abstracting From Real-life Situations into Bureaucratic Categories

The concrete individual — with his or her motivations, formative contexts, narrative history, standpoint — is not really present at the Welfare interview.[103] (This effect is similar to Configuration "A," but in accord with a bureaucratic rather than a moralizing logic.) Likewise, the concrete community — with its spontaneous existential feel — is not present. Humans are being fitted into an abstract, cognitive and "worldless" set of classifications. Before analyzing the features of the abstracting propensity of bureaucracies from the standpoint of the poor, we should note the sheer scale and complexity of the system that rises up before the client.

---

[102] Miller, "Poverty and respect."

[103] Benhabib ("The Generalized," 160) suggests, reviewing Gilligan's research, that women tend to resist the abstraction of people from their concrete motivations and relational contexts—tending to favour the standpoint of the "concrete other." In the bureaucracy, then, they are being processed by an especially uncongenial "masculine" mentality.

The processing of particular cases involves placing them into categories and subcategories to which legal and policy directives apply, and which confer entitlements and benefits on the client, from whom precise and verified data must be gathered. This immense chain of paper and electronic information must be channelled from application forms and caseworker files to central offices and computers — which inevitably takes time and is subject to administrative error, all of which is painful for the poor to endure. For Unemployment Insurance (UI) the waiting period of at least three weeks seems lengthy to the client, Suzette comments, but it allows processing and file review time. They are always trying to "improve paper flow ... to make it more speed-efficient." Improved in-house technology has meant that they do not send everything elsewhere to be processed as before.

Margaret admits that the huge, unwieldy nature of her organization generates dysfunctions and disincentives: "Our systems are too complex. It's hard sometimes for people who work in the system to understand it, let alone clients understanding it ... . Forms could be simplified, processes could be simplified." She made the valuable point that, if she as a *worker* finds a form too complex, "I'm not going to try to explain it to the client. I'm going to kind of say, 'That's the way it is.' And that is natural, but it doesn't help." The system discourages dialogue.

Abstraction as Tunnel Vision

In her official chair, formulating from within her institutional perspective and voice, Suzette seemed not to accept the category of "poverty" or to see the holistic problems of low-income people. She did not know whether UI claimants who were suffering hardship during their minimum three-week waiting period would qualify for welfare — implying that it was not in her bailiwick. When asked the question, "Do you see UI and poverty as interconnected?," she did not answer from a empathetic location in the real world, but preferred to invoke the rhetoric of social insurance:

> It shouldn't be. The whole concept of unemployment insurance is to avoid it. The reason we insure anything is to prevent a large financial loss when something happens ... [I]t's a shared risk and we pay into it so that if something does happen we have that financial protection to sort of bridge the gap between jobs. So I see it as more of a positive course.

When reminded by the interviewer of the fact that benefit levels are kept at lower levels for poorer claimants, so that UI will not pull them out of poverty, she answered: "Yes, it won't correct it. You're quite right, it won't correct if there is an economic imbalance." When asked if UI will address this "imbalance," she said "No." Suzette sounds (categorically) naive and compartmentalizing, as she resorts to easy rhetoric about the ostensible purpose of UI in the teeth of the economic chaos caused by joblessness. Helping the poor by improving their economic situation is not her main interest; that just moves the poor from this pocket to that pocket. She is more enthusiastic about the new emphasis on turning UI funds to training purposes. There is a tunnel vision here, and the language ("economic imbalance") is technocratic, floating over the surface of lives who in their real condition need benefit dollars to survive.

Both the bureaucratic and political logics of government run systematically against the real-world interests of poor people, according to a housing specialist named Chris. He considers that housing (especially low-cost permanent housing integrated into most parts of the city) and jobs are basic to the well-being of the poor. But the bureaucrats do not see housing as a living issue, only a cheque or a shelter cost. Ignoring their fundamental importance puts government in the position of simply supplying bandaids and, of course, covering the many deficits stemming from inappropriate housing. As well, *political* logics serve poor people's housing and other community needs poorly. Provincial politicians do not supply the money that is needed for an area but rather give just a little bit here and there to placate the largest number of constituencies. Community organizing, for Chris, is the only viable way for the problems to be researched, identified and politicized.

Distributional Injustices

The UI counsellors and insurance officers apply many rules which defend the fund against so-called ineligible claimants. They should look at the real-world effects of these exclusions. Dan, from the low-income sample, experiences bitter poverty with his partner Sandra. He paid into UI in his various marginal jobs and, when he was jobless, was informed by UI that he was ineligible because he had helped his partner who is the superintendent of a public

housing complex. The couple felt furious and disentitled because
of this rejection, as illustrated by this excerpt from their interview.

SANDRA: They literally denied him UIC because he was helping
          me with these buildings.

DANIEL: I was being truthful to the government.

SANDRA: And if he'd lied he'd have got the damn thing.

DANIEL: And then this is the thanks I get from the government
          by being truthful. They denied my money. So what
          am I supposed to do? I'm powerless. I don't know
          where else to go.

SANDRA: Don't worry; something will come up in the end.

DANIEL: That little money that government's holding back. The
          UIC they're holding back would help her and I a little
          bit more to step a little further.

SANDRA: It would certainly help put cash in our pockets, that's
          for sure.

DANIEL: That's right.

SANDRA: It would help get the bills paid. It would help keep
          food in this house.

The technocratic decision was made in ignorance of the impact on
the "powerless" Dan and Sandra, whose life context made the
decision distributionally unjust.

The real-world and distributional illogic of differentiating benefit
levels according to how deserving or non-deserving clients are
judged to be is attacked by Angela, an official with Community
Legal Aid. To her "it just doesn't make any sense" for someone on
general social assistance to be given lower benefits because they
are thought to be less deserving than someone on family benefits,
when their survival needs are the same. Her point is simple. When
you are allocating for basic needs on General Welfare Assistance
(GWA) then what you give them should be *adequate to their basic
needs* and not held artificially low because GWA claimants are not
as deserving as Family Benefits Assistance (FBA) claimants. All these
bureaucratic discriminations actually mandate poverty. Meagre
social wages, kept low according to the reference points of poor
market wages or the benefit levels of the "more deserving,"
perpetuate needfulness and primes the pump of the "helping" and

admininstering systems. Adequate social wages would put much of the public (anti-pauperist) machinery out of commission.

From the standpoint of the poor, the benefits that are the least costly to the self — which construe them as rights-bearers and consumers rather than dependents — are the most stingily unresponsive to real-world need, especially of women. These benefits are given out as compensation that is proportional to the larger premiums paid and the greater number of years worked. For example, the disability pension is based on numbers of years worked and the number of credits earned and can be quite generous. But Louise, a divorced woman of 58 on a $500-a-month disability pension, insisted that everyone should be treated the same "because the expenses are the same." In another older woman's case, that of Ann, the heritage of a lifetime of minimum wage can be seen in her meagre Old Age Security (OAS) and Canada Pension of $582 a month. The poor, especially women, who are marginal to the labour market, can expect their marginality to continue on social wages, which are often of the more discretionary kind. There is a decidedly patriarchal cast to the rationality of bureaucracy as well as the distibutional biases of its benefits.

Wielding Discretion

Despite our belief in universal citizenship rights, in reality they have to be applied. As Martin Hewitt indicates, "these rights are often indeterminate and, in practice, not always universally guaranteed."[104] Discretion has to be wielded. As we have noted, the social service bureaucracy processes diverse human situations according to a system of typifications to which rules and benefits apply. But the client here brings forward not an easily verifiable item — like a driver's license to the Ministry of Transportation — but a story of need which has to be authenticated. Human details turn up in these stories which defy categories and outpace rulemaking, and every day discretionary judgments must be made. Eventually these discrepancies take on patterns, or attract political attention, and they affect policies. As Alan Wolfe pointed out,

---

[104] Hewitt, *Welfare, Ideology and Need*, 31.

"society ... is a process, not a thing, oscillating between rules that establish behaviour and behavior that establishes rules."[105]

Now we have seen that the scope of discretion is very large for the givers of charity. The bureaucratic official's discretion is also considerable — in the manner and pacing of dealings with the client, in the power to manipulate and threaten, and in the ability to advocate for and encourage the client. The scope is narrower, however, than Configuration "A," circumscribed as it is by entitlement rules deriving from legislation and policy directives. Indeed, in the bureaucratic field, the two poles of "entitlement" and "discretion" mark out a terrain wherein interests of provider and client are accommodated and struggled over. For instance, before a change in policy in 1988, Family Benefits workers monitored their single mother clients for telltale signs of a "spouse in the house," and homes were watched for evidence of a male visitor staying over. Women's groups and others lobbied for a change and, finally, succeeded. Shifts in mores occur, but rule changes may take years to reflect them.

One official affirmed strongly that "regulations should not prescribe relationships" and judged as inappropriate the discretionary penalties that followed from older "moral violations." She, and other educated professionals in social services, are less likely to accept the moralistic and negative associations that cling to the public image of the poor. For instance, she felt the "tremendous pressure in the community around all of these people on Welfare that are spending their money on ... beer." Her own attitude is blunt and non-jugmental:

> Why shouldn't poor people drink? Like I don't think that means anything. So what if they all go and spend money on beer. If I was trying and struggling to get by, I might spend more money on beer myself.

So the public thinks the poor should spend money on clothes or food but what if, after months and months of doing that, the low-income person wants to have some fun. The official challenges the public watchdogs: "What right do you have to tell somebody because they're poor they should not drink? Is that one of your

---

[105] Wolfe, *Whose Keeper?*, 214.

values, that poor people ought not to drink, ought not to smoke?" She then levels a good, bureaucratically rational question. If a poor person does an inappropriate thing and is noticed, "does that mean that our system should be designed to somehow make sure that everybody is not going to act like that?" She concedes that some low-income people behave badly, just like some rich people, but disagrees that they should "be held up as examples of exactly why our system has to be maintained."

Still, the Welfare system lags behind changes in mores and contains immense rigidities. The interviewer asked Margaret about a young woman whose benefits were reduced because the man she was living with had a full-time job (with a low income). They were a common-law couple, but she valued her self-reliance and did not want to change the nature of their relationship by becoming his dependent. The regulation cutting down her benefits was shaping the couple's life in the house in a way that made her resentful. Margaret was asked if that has changed.

> In some situations, yes, and in some situations, no. The way the regulations now stand, that could still be an issue ... I think that could still be an issue.

So regulations *do* prescribe relationships, once again in a patriarchal direction, but the client gets to choose her type of patriarchy — private or public. Whatever the liberality of attitude at the top, Welfare will continue to keep a sharp eye on potential providers other than itself.

With that background, we ask: what are the enabling and constraining aspects of our service providers' use of discretion?

Discretion Which Enables

The caseworker can become an advocate for the client in trying to gain satisfaction in the complex bureaucracy. Margaret admitted that the system often ran against the interests of the person: "Our system does a heck of a lot of things that really work the wrong way for the people, and I think that's true." Faced with this systemic dysfunction, she thought the caseworker could be an in-house "advocate," helping the client "use the system in the best way ... They have to help the client to negotiate that maze of bureaucracy to get the best out of it." But this takes time, and this facilitative task may degrade into mere style as the worker's caseload grows and she loses a sense of the client's particularity. But there is a bigger contradiction, which may take the form of a role conflict for the worker. Unlike advocates out in the community who help low-income persons to cope with external forces (such as landlords, employers, etc.), the caseworker tries to be an enabler in a system in which she is also a controller. The worker constantly bumps into the limits of her enablement; i.e., the disciplinary or control requirements of the system. As Margaret said: "We have to do our best to do both — [on the one hand,] we have to try to meet our accountability ... to ensure that people are looking for work and, on the other hand, try to positively support them to do that ... [This] can have quite a different thrust, and it can be a conflict for the system."

A caring manner may empower a client but, in a busy organization, the caring of the social service official may easily descend into superficial mannerism. After all the system is often dehumanizing — controlling people, giving them inadequate funds, invading their privacy — and being "nice" can make the worker feel good. She may feel that she is empowering the client — but more often than not her manners are allowing *her* to come to terms with the obstacles, not the client. Furthermore, caring may be more available higher up in the organization or in the complex cases, where time can be taken. Sensitivity is often shown at the special counsellor's desk, or the director's desk, when the case is so complex that normal procedures cannot handle it. The vast majority of cases, however, are subject to powerful forces of flow-through, where niceness is occasionally genuine but often is a thin lubricant for interpersonal interaction.

Discretion Which Constrains and Controls

Service providers and critics from the community-building role configuration ("D") find that the London social service bureaucracy is overly strict and conservative with clients. Let us look to its city council. The province gives Welfare regulations and guidelines but leaves some discretion to the municipal councils. Welfare, being one of the largest departments in the city government, is under steady pressure by a fiscally conservative city council to cut costs. This form of community discretion can starve good programs for funds not because the programs are not needed or sound but

because rate-payers' interests in minimizing taxes are more politically influential than the interests of the poor. (Community discretion of the cost-cutting variety can feed into case discretion used
by the worker whose approach to the client may be aversive rather
than accommodating; e.g., "Why should I give you scarce public
funds?"). The council's refusal of Welfare program funding requests
is usually cloaked in arguments that some other governmental
jurisdiction should take care of this service, not Welfare. Margaret
alluded to this game of "political football" when she commented:

> [S]ome of that gets tied up with who should pay for it — not
> whether or not the service is a good idea, but this is costing us
> way too much ... [D]iscretion ends up getting used in a way that
> might be seen — if you're only looking at it from the client's point
> of view — as something that can be used another way.

From the standpoint of the client, she is saying that political choices
are being made against their interests in the arena of city politics.

Familism

Another discretionary area has to do with the new right's attempt
to devolve welfare responsibilities from state workers to family and
volunteers (or, unpaid women caretakers). Margaret worries that if
we let the state care for our elderly and teenagers, "is it taking our
society in the direction where that becomes the expectation, and it
weakens further our sense of responsibility towards each other?"
Her concern is that people will think "I don't need to take care of
my mother (or child), because there's a system that will." — and
that this will weaken the family. But we must raise both a class and
gender subtext to this concern of hers. First, it must be asked, is
the family's inability to care for its members a function of its
callousness or neglect *or* of externally determined poverty of
resources? In the latter situation, when market income is not there,
the mutual dependency of family members may be debilitating for
individuals who need the state to help shoulder their own burden
and that of the family member needing care. A bad economy may
be more destructive of the family than a generous social safety net.
Furthermore, is Margaret similarly worried about rich people having
their old relatives institutionalized or their children taken care of by
nannies or boarding schools? Does she worry about the decline of
the family among the affluent?

The gender issue is also present here. When an older person is receiving family care, it is less likely that he or she will receive it from statutory state services. Who are the family carers, but women? Making the family "more responsible" means increasing the unpaid caring work of women in a stable family (i.e., with male breadwinner, wife, dependents) — with the effect of making women more dependent upon men than upon the market or state.[106]

Handling Appeals In-House

One official wants to increase the zone of discretion within the system, rather than being subject to legal challenges from such adversarial systems as Legal Aid and the courts. Appeals should be coped with by staff members and the administrator, who would adapt the system in the light of the appeals. Why not externalize the appeal process? Because, the official answered, the worker feels undermined, and you may end up with a less caring system. She went on to say that if appeals within the office are well responded to, then the client has a countervailing power to the caseworker's. "If the client feels that the only way they are going to get anything fair from our system is by complaining to somebody from the outside, it doesn't give much hope for the future in terms of the client's dealing with the system." There is a huffy, paternalistic note here that reinforces the common finding of the study that empathy and caring has its price — in this case, the expectation that you will merge with the organization and its control and public relations apparatus. "If I care for you" carries the reciprocal expectation, "you will be unpolitical."

Social Patriarchy — The Jealous State

There is considerable power held by officials over long-term aid recipients. Mothers on Family Benefits (and people on long-term disability) are considered, from the vantage point of the labour market, "inactive segments" of the population. They are compensated not from employment wages but "instead from legal titles and support claims that are not based on labour contracts."[107] What

[106] Lewis, "Chapter 6: Introduction," 134.

[107] Offe, *Disorganized Capitalism*, 26.

enables them to stay outside the labour market is their recourse to
the family *or* the public system (the emphasis on "or" added by
public officials). Barred from excessive man-watching by law,
Family Benefits workers still, according to single parent Stephanie,
"watch the company you keep."

Stephanie received a strong dose of negative discretion which
took on a "social patriarchal" form.[108] When she lived in Ottawa,
her Family Benefits worker called her home on one of the few days
when her ex-husband was seeing his children, having been granted
visitation. He answered the phone and the worker hung up
immediately. Later the worker demanded that Stephanie come to
an 8 a.m. meeting, or she would have her Mother's Allowance
benefits cut off. The first question the enraged worker asked her
was, "Well, who was the man that was with you?" The government
official acted here like a spurned lover. For all the impersonal style
of her institution, the official here betrayed her true discretionary
attitude; obviously she considered the single-parent enclave as
"government property" which has been staked out in a moral claim.
It is as though subsidized members of the single mother enclave
are virtually married to the government — and no rival supporter
will be countenanced.

The Construction of Female Clients

As we have seen, the genders are subjectified differently in the
Welfare system and have different levels of negative discretion.[109]
The beneficiaries of the masculine-oriented social insurance
schemes are less stigmatized and are seen as rights-bearers. After
all, they have paid into their schemes in partnership with their
employers and thus are felt to have a right to their benefits. Being
less administered or in receipt of in-kind benefits, they have cash
to use on the marketplace as consumers and possessive individuals.
By contrast, clients in the feminine sector of the welfare system
receive benefits that are non-contributory — come out of tax
revenues — and are often set by the state to be some portion of

[108] Ursel, "The State."

[109] Fraser, "Women, Welfare," 151.

the poverty line (usually one-half to three-quarters). A high degree of eligibility monitoring and surveillance comes with these benefits, many of which are in-kind. These women are not situated as rights-bearers but as dependent recipients of government largesse. Being stigmatized as non-working state burdens, these women are often disciplined by compulsory work-fare arrangements.

A service provider at a woman's shelter, Monique, commented on the state's mixed signals to the mother conveyed by the too-low social wage. "If you say to this woman, 'We approve of your wanting to stay home with your children at this age and not go out to work, but you can only have this much money to do it on,' it's a pretty hard message that you are giving and it sure isn't due to their sinfulness or poor moral standards that they've stepped down into poverty." She is correct because the poverty is state-maintained and the needfulness is fashioned into an administrable shape.

The system is trying to construct Stephanie's identity, or self-relation, to conform to its rules. More than an application of rules, it is an imposition of rules on life such that life is moulded in bureaucratically legitimate forms. When on family benefits, mother and children are constructed as a "household," and any mutual aid extending beyond that official unit is held in suspicion. But the main construction here is the low-income woman as *mother*. It may be helpful to formulate the system's mixed message to the person as a discourse: "We will provide you with this family benefit on conditions that deny your sexual access to men.[110] Since we do not offer day care, decent job training, or a job that pays enough to support a family, then obviously we are constructing you entirely as mothers. Your needs will be interpreted as maternal needs and your benefits kept so low that you will feel guilty if you spend the money on yourself, instead of your children." The first message could lead to a respect for the mother role, but it is combined with a second, conflicting message: "You have no right to a decent social wage that will allow you to develop yourself as a person. We mistrust you, because you probably desire to live off others as well as the state. We will invade your privacy and shape your decisions in system-conforming ways." "In effect," Fraser comments, "it

---

[110] Connell, "States, powers," 6.

decrees simultaneously that these women must be and yet cannot be normative mothers."[111]

The Ambiguity of Job Developers

One way of freeing up the enabling function with respect to employment is to lodge it in workers other than the powerful caseworkers with their rule-bound eligibility mandate. Hence the Job Development Program at Welfare, which was ostensibly intended to provide constructive job-finding assistance to employable clients, rather than simply apply the punitive sanctions. Job developers deal primarily with how to connect people to jobs in the community. What are the barriers towards employment for the client and how can they be overcome? How can the planning process become more realistic — in terms of targeted wage levels, for instance? (One official thought that many young people are presenting the Job Developers with expectations of jobs at $10 an hour, which shows her that they are the products of an affluent society. That gives us an idea that the wage level that Welfare will push for among its clients, and will support out in the labour market, will be closer to minimum wage.)

This new service provider role of job developer has its enabling features. It keeps a distance — though never severs its tie — from the rule-enforcing "paymasters" elsewhere in the organization. It can clear away inefficiencies in the job search and enhance personal skill. But its enabling thrust comes up against two constraints or rigidities. First, Welfare is something of a "hot plate" for employables. Pressure to take the current job on offer is strong and also legislated. As one official put it, "We don't care whether you like the job or not; if you're physically capable of doing it, you're supposed to take it ... That's what the Act says, so that's what the caseworker is trying to enforce." This constraint reduces the job developer enablement to quick preparation for the available jobs rather than a more thorough preparation for a life free of poverty.

The second constraint is the fact that the current jobs available to people on social assistance, and those laid off in the recession, are low-paying, insecure jobs in the service sector. The welfare

---

[111] Fraser, "Women, Welfare," 153.

bureaucracy's attempt to reduce the welfare caseload, coupled with its staffing shortages, leads to a pressure for employables to take those jobs. How will the job developer handle the conflict when he/she realizes that the barriers to employment often are erected not out of the personal deficiencies of the client but from the characteristics of the bad jobs on offer? The job developer's hoped-for assistance for the client's climb out of poverty, which is virtually thwarted by the welfare organization's imperatives and the unpromising job environment, risks ending in cynicism, with-drawal, or a curtailed enablement. (There are gender-oppressive effects of the compulsory placements known as "workfare," which "function to subsidize employers of low-wage 'women's work' in the service sector and thus to reproduce the sex-segmented, dual labour market."[112])

Conclusion

There are legislative entitlements to goods and services which the poor have gained in the welfare state, and these are a source of power, albeit defensive, for low-income people. There are enabling features of life on Family Benefits, for instance, which aid women in raising their children in better material conditions than would be otherwise possible. Case discretion can be exercised with sensitivity and humanity. (In Chapter 8, we will show how much people are helped by certain government interventions.)

But being "on the system" (to use people's everyday term) is mostly disempowering. Social wages almost never take people out of poverty. Their levels are not negotiated with the recipients, such that they reflect real-world needs. The welfare budget is the whipping boy of cost-cutters. City councillors, rate-payers and angry citizens press for cuts in benefits and services, as well as higher levels of monitoring and surveillance. The levels are pegged in reference to the lowest market wage and are well below the poverty line. As an example of the inadequacy of social assistance rates, the following are the maximum amounts available per day to recipients for such expenses as food, clothing, furniture, personal

---

[112] Fraser, "Women, Welfare," 146.

and household supplies, telephone, transportation, and remaining shelter costs:[113]

- Mothers and 2 small children — $5.83 per person, per day;
- Parent and 1 teenager — $7.98 per person, per day;
- Single Adult — $6.41 per person, per day.

These low levels of income *guarantee* further dependence on the system, the charities, or family members — or people simply do without. In most cases, the poor are constructed as stigmatized sub-citizens, needing to be watched by a self-righteous community. The anti-pauperist project, though qualified by some entitlements, is still an formative influence on the rules and discretionary guidance of service providers, especially in the treatment of women on long-term benefits.

The communitarian service provider, Colleen, combined these themes in her statement of hope for the people in the public-housing project she serves:

> If there could be some sort of system that would remove the degradation of having to relate to a Welfare worker, having to queue up at Christmas for hampers, of feeling that your soul belongs to the bureaucracy of the province of Ontario, and everything that you do has to be reported and on paper and you're afraid to do things for yourself and therefore your self-esteem is lower ...

The panoptic principle of inspectability and the need for discipline for "deviants" or "shirkers" of market reality continue to be applied in state encounters with the poor everyday.

We conclude by noting a more macrosocial aspect of state power: that it wants to expand its influence in the community assessment of needs and wants to pull the strings of the micro-agencies servicing these needs. Needs is a growth industry.

> Community forums are comparatively economical and they provide policy planners and agency administrators with an opportunity to gauge the views of those who have fallen into the "underserved" or "non-served" category in the community. They stimulate the identification of social service needs and provide those responsible for needs assessment with an opportunity, not

---

[113] Ad Hoc Collective, "Some cuts don't heal."

only to hear from many ... but also to identify those participants
and agencies most interested in resolving them.[114]

While we applaud the widening of the communication channels to
the state, scepticism may be appropriate here. Given the pervasive
disempowerment of the poor "on the system," given the fact that
the economy has failed to provide adequate incomes for the poor,
are we to take seriously the expansion of the bureaucratic helping
machinery to record yet more needs and to establish yet more
services? What part of this expansionary dynamic of needs assessment is a make-work project for the professional middle class who
will move its small grants and studies from this corner to that of an
impoverished civil realm? Are not those who want an end to *poverty,*
not pauperism, entitled to scepticism?

We now turn to a role configuration of service providers who
are not social service bureaucrats, but who formulate their mission
as responding to the needs of the poor.

---

[114] Culpitt, *Welfare and Citizenship,* 172.

5

"C": Needs Responding

*A*ll service provider informants tried to meet people's needs but, for some, it became a defining configuring mode. These included workers in legal aid services, a youth shelter, a soup kitchen, men's and women's hostels or missions, and a family consultant service with the police force. This is a mode of help-giving — in fairly structured and artificial environments — which responds to low-income individuals who approach and claim to need help or are referred by others. People's troubles present themselves to providers in controlled settings, not naturalistically in their native environments. To the provider, particular need calls out for a particular service response.

Less abstractive than the charity givers and bureaucratic subsidizers, this approach is sensitive to a social-psychological and interpersonal *situation*. The originating poor situation is thought to be a kind of chamber setting where psychosocial deficits are played out in stressful interpersonal relations. The provider hopes to repair the casualties of such situations and, in some cases, to provide a therapeutic alternative space in which to rebuild the client's belief in self and others.

The perspectives in this "C" configuration on our basic issues of need, help, empowerment, are extremely diverse — sometimes using charity, social service and justice models. The voice of the provider is multivocal, reflecting as it does empathy with a wide spectrum of human suffering and humanity. Providers waver from a personalistic types-of-individual analysis to a individual-within-situation emphasis. Absorbed as they are in lifestyle problems enacted in situations, they are less inclined to see the formative collective influences of *community* or *society*, either as generators or eliminators of poverty. The emphasis on empathy causes an impaired vision of power differentials, which are maintained in this mode but euphemized and softened. The power of the provider is not reflexively grasped or articulated, nor is the power that manifests itself from the mouths and discourse of improving subjects.

Once again, the self-presentation of the service provider along with its linked accorded definition of low-income clients will be depicted, especially as they are woven into interchanges of caring and power. The needs responder constructs the other as a person with needs — for help, space and structure. The constitutive practices of this mode are two: ministering to needs and providing a re-integrative space.

Ministering to Needs

The needs focus can be on individuals, families, communities, or the society — so configuration "C" often shades into role "D" (community) and "E" (societal). For most of the providers in the study, the focus is individual, family, street life, and referral services.

To get a sense of the range of poor people's troubles which present themselves to service providers, we can introduce Patricia's drop-in centre and shelter for (mostly) young street people. Her husband is an ex-motorcyclist with a hard life, who became a born-again Christian. This man decided to open a drop-in centre for street kids in trouble who mistrusted the conventional agencies. Some of the young people are burnt out after going from foster home to foster home. At the time of the interview, Patricia was bringing clothes to a 15-year-old street girl being held in custody. The girl had been on the street since she was 13 and was into drugs, alcohol and prostitution. She suffered from chronic pelvic infections from sexual promiscuity. Patricia had taken the girl into her own home for a time to help sort out her life and get her off the streets. Other people who came to her drop-in centre were ex-psychiatric patients, who were released from hospital psychiatric wards with no group work and no follow-up. She had dealt with suicidal people, incest victims and, in one case, a mentally disturbed young woman who had severely abused her baby. The woman had had no follow-up and no person or groups to fall back on. "These mistakes are walking around," Patricia noted, suggesting that smaller agencies handle the neglected people from bigger institutions.

Here are some of the problems encountered by the service providers in the "C" configuration:

- Temporary homelessness, due to eviction (money ran out), transiency;
- People who have lost their wife, home, job;
- Young people with poor parenting models and dysfunctional families;
- Illiteracy, mental health problems, drug or alcohol addictions;
- Lifelong acquaintance with the ills of poverty;
- Sexual (and other) abuse in childhood leading to dysfunctional people/families;
- People on disabilities, including learning disabilities;
- Anorexia, bulimia;
- Schizophrenics, often requiring monitoring of medications.

Some of these providers have a deep awareness of and empathy with the victimization of poor people. One service provider, named Monique, works in an emergency shelter for women and families. Her account of an abused woman who was no longer supported by her husband and who had moved out into the community on Welfare deserves close attention:

> [T]o cope not only with the residual effect of separation and independence, rather than submission and dependence, ... [but also] coping with poverty is just devastating. To have nothing, to maybe have actually had a personal income that provided for a whole lot of stuff that you walked out and left behind. [T]o start with, all your personal goods are donated if you can't access them from home. All your furniture is from Goodwill or the Sally or it's all second-hand and you probably come from a much more affluent background. Your housing doesn't have good locks on the doors, it doesn't have good heat, it's in a scary neighbourhood, there's scary people around.

She then paints us a picture of the financial strains of the woman's first month.

> The first month your income is just going to run out because — you know yourself — in setting up a new place for the very first time, you got to get staples. That's the month you buy your flour, your sugar and so on. You do that and there's nothing left, there's nothing left. So they're knocking on ... doors for the food bank and then there are all the food sources, and it is humiliating and it is frightening. And for a abused woman who has been trying so hard to salvage her self image, [which she had felt] as worthless and no good.

Then, the money having run out, the woman can decide that it is too much and returns to her husband. Or, being penniless, she is evicted and ends up at Monique's shelter. "She hits a brick wall all the time," Monique concludes, and we know exactly and painfully what she means.

Types of Responding and Caring

The range of help is enormous. Young people are taught to handle their babies and pick up general parenting skills. At his rehab organization, Jacob helps the men with "the mechanics of living, of coping." If a man wants to know or do something beyond his capability, "it's best that I go to a person and the person shows me how ... And I can understand it better." Jacob tries to get books into the hands of the poor, especially their children. In other agencies, legal aid is provided for a number of circumstances — if the client's benefit cheque is reduced, or there are overpayment problems, or if he or she has been denied benefits altogether. One agency has staff that knows the housing market well and can help women access the housing registry and the London Housing authority if need be.

Much of the work is front-line sizing up of problems and referring the person to the agency that is specially equipped to handle the difficulty. The agencies are often entry points and liaisons for troubled individuals so that they can enter a more complex institutional grid of legal advocacy clinics, as well as medical, legal, educational, addiction, and therapeutic counselling services. People are connected with Alcoholics Anonymous, Alanon, Changing Ways (for abusive men), Victim Witness program, Battered Women's Advocacy Clinic, and so on. As the Community Legal Aid worker, Angela, indicated: "We try to work on being that unintimidating point to the legal system to be able to ask questions that you don't know where to phone to get an answer."

I want to look now in more detail at the modes of engagement, both psychological and institutional, that the providers adopt.

Psychologically Engaged: The Exemplar Role

Jacob is an older, respected official in a men's hostel, which accommodates and tries to rehabilitate homeless and destitute men. He has a two-pronged approach to help: (a) what you need and how we can help; and (b) how you can help yourself or what can you take ownership or responsibility for? The second is the more psychologically complex and subtly discloses a personal transaction the provider is offering. Jacob and other personally invested "C workers" take pride in being less impersonal and more welcoming than "B" services. The questions asked are less bureaucratic, true, but they are also more probing — for they furnish the material for *empathy*, which is the prize in this form of helping. What is Jacob's understanding of empathy? "Empathy isn't best projected; it's something that's there. If you project it, it's phony." So he thinks that it is empathy, more than compassion, which makes the difference with the client from the very start. The empathy is not a mannerism but a part of the helper's personal relationship with the poor. There is an agenda here which merits examination.

Jacob emphasizes personal responsibility, which is a latent power covered up by poverty and addiction which the worker wants to unlock. He tells us that he wants to know the dreams of the men and what makes them tick. But is not the personal power idea fraught with difficulties? Telling men who have experienced abuse as children, or hard times due to psychological problems, disabilities, or persistent joblessness, that "you can do it if you try," is a risky, potentially misleading endeavour — especially if it is generalized as a strategy for low-income people as a whole (Jacob is an honoured figure among the charities and social services).

Furthermore, who's empowering whom? The strategy risks becoming so self-indulgent and self-involving as to transgress the autonomy of the other. The pursuit of empathy (surely worthier, it is thought, than quizzing them on incomes and assets) gives permission to hook one's self-realizing project with the client's interpreted project. We can appreciate Jacob's curiosity and insight and humanity, but this notion of humane and creative tinkering with clients' psyches, even with the clients' ownership, does not create the space and boundaries needed to hear poor people's concerns. It fails to address the hard realities outside of the provider-client horizon; i.e., economic-structural issues which create problems and generate trouble in people's lives.

He uses his own life as a model for the fallen men in his organization. In his youth, Jacob had "been in cities without money. In Montreal, I stayed in a mission; I slept under bridges." His own struggle upward is both credential of authenticity (giving him prestige among the helpers who have known hard times themselves) and model for the men. He counsels service providers: just be real. "The real treatment is in the individual. The medicine is in the person, not the mechanics. I'm the medicine [laughs]. This could give you a swell head; that's the cause of all these Messiahs." Jacob is an artist as a helper, playing on his own and the other's capacity for transformation. He sees himself as "working with the poor," as opposed to "helping the poor." Fundamentally, he sees the poor as driven by personal deficits, which become his mandate. Lacking a compass, the men wander into the rehab centre and find, in Jacob's life, their "true North," their positive reference point. This humane and self-knowing helper, by no means monolithic in his helping modes, defines his interest succinctly. To repeat his words from an earlier chapter: "We're fulfilling our own needs, as well, in helping the poor. This is how we get our kicks."

The Helper as Institutionally Engaged (Advocate)

The self-conceptions of these service providers' roles vary along a continuum from professional advocacy at one end (e.g., community legal services) to neutral provision of help on the other (e.g., the soup kitchen). Some providers take up ambivalent middle positions, practising advocacy on behalf of the low-income person at times, but with a nervous eye on the funder.

Taking the professional advocate role first, we have the statement of Angela, a lawyer with a neighbourhood legal aid clinic:

> [W]e are businesses to advocate on behalf of clients ... both on
> an individual basis and on a broader basis by having involvement
> in community education and in law reform projects.

The community education part having been curtailed due to understaffing, most of her time is spent on individual cases. The individual part of her mandate is, of course, very important. She represents low-income people in disputes with landlords and the Unemployment Insurance and Welfare bureaucracies. Her form of advocacy on behalf of the client, then, is a kind of figure/ground reversal of the bureaucratic form of provision, whose point of reference is more the system than the client. There is also a community, as well as a lawyerly, link with the people they serve in that low-income persons sit on their board of directors. "This helps us keep our feet on the ground in terms of understanding what our client community's concerns are." This allows her to set her approach off from the more system-oriented Role B, even though there are bureaucratic similarities.

In the middle of the continuum, service providers are hesitant and somewhat ambivalent about advocating for their people. Doris is a worker with the family consultant service that is under the wing of the police department. She and other workers go out to help calm the combatants in domestic disputes, whether in advance of or along with the arrival of police. When asked if she was ever in conflict with her role as adjunct of the police force and helper of abused partners, she said "yes" emphatically. Are you free, she was then asked, to advocate for the client, perhaps against the grain of the police handling of the case? She indicated that they subtly keep citizens informed of the ways they can get proper help and representation, but "advocate too much and we'd be gone." Her service is considered a "frill" by some police administrators, and these are often the first to be cut when police budgets are constrained.

Helper as Neutral or Disengaged

Sister Laureen at the soup kitchen — which is neutral regarding advocacy but communal in its intent — wants to be open to the needy whatever their need may be: food, friendship, the warmth and sounds of a room full of people. There is no screening process. The religious sisters that run the soup kitchen in this communal way are determined that people not feel or be judged. They wanted volunteers who, apart from cooking, would feel comfortable with low-income people, who do not judge but are there because they want to be. One can see, in this elective community, that all persons, providers and recipients, are to share the common ethos.

Kenneth — a help-giver with the Christian Army with a predominantly moralistic cast (see Chapter 3) — does not see his role as an advocate or placard-carrier, but rather as someone just doing his job. "No, I wouldn't say we're an advocate type thing. We are trying to provide the best that we can for them. We're not out carrying placards complaining about what the government is doing or not doing type-of-thing. What we're trying to do is do our job better ... It's what we're doing; how can we improve what we are doing?"

Kenneth's helping style is mixed. Ideally, he would want to monitor and coordinate the poor's consumption and to counsel them.

Even the heavily self-invested service providers — whether religious, political, humanistic — devote a good amount of time to simply helping and meeting needs. In some cases, perhaps Kenneth's, the helping mode is a kind of default mode for providers when the more involving strategies fail or are resisted. In most, it may be just wanting to do the thing required, wanting to be useful. For Jacob, the criterion of eligibility is: "Do you need shelter? Do you need something to eat? Do you need clothing?" Later, he commented: "When we use the word 'care,' we use a fairly broad description — giving thread to sew a button, or razor blades, advice, more than advice actually, some help in applying for some of the income security programs ... [The care is] practical, dealing with the here and now, dealing with the mechanics of a community and how to work their way through ... red tape."

Providing a Re-integrative Space

Some of the needs responders try to furnish a space where low-income people can recompose themselves after being fractured by the experiences of poverty and of other service providers. Hopefully these individuals will feel like persons again, not wards of the state or untrustworthy children. Their days will be structured, and they will be invited to relate with others along quasi-familial lines — with staff as mentors or parent-figures, and peers as siblings. If possible, they will be recognized and counselled and safe.

In describing the positive space they offer, the needs responders contrasted it with abstract bureaucratic space. There is a palpable disgust with the human coldness of bureaucracy. In Jacob's words:

> Get rid of, or at least weaken, the bureaucracy. These terrible offices, where you have to go to counters and have people look at you and say, "Well, what do you want?" They're good people, but they're only hired to fill out forms.

He is against "means testing and hoop jumping." Similarly, Patricia at her street mission described her group's ability to handle time-consuming cases: "I'm allowed to care. I don't have to treat them as a case file, or just as a client ... [Our group is not] locked into categories." She resisted the way the bureaucracy refers to persons as "clients" but, having to deal with government, she had to use their terms. Her humanism bridled against the bureaucracy's conversion of persons and their needs into categories. "People get so busy worrying about using the right terms for things that they forget about the person they are dealing with. That the person isn't terms and is a human being." She took pride in her organization's readiness to meet needs even well into the night. Street Aid offers a more informal, accepting environment for people such as pregnant teenagers who are scared and have been "agencied to death."

Why such venom in the descriptions of bureaucracy? There is certainly constructive empathy into the impersonal manner and daunting complexity that are presented to low-income people in trouble. But, as well, smaller agencies find themselves drawn into compromises when they accept Welfare's per diem rates or become dependent on government contract funding. They become bureaucratized themselves. This is more monitoring and less client advocacy. Even Jacob's organization has changed from "no questions asked, open door" to a place of rules and screening methods. Some of his own staff have become "professional" in the cold, distancing sense that Jacob dislikes. There is a threat of a loss of identity and organizational culture by these changes, which may turn them gradually into "privately administered public agencies."[115]

Safe, Fewer Hassles, Structure

The space offered to the overburdened low-income person is safer and less pressuring than the outside. A woman told Monique that the women's hostel helped her straighten out her life; she felt safe there. In the service provider's words, "the pressure is off finally, and it's a respite ... and it's a lot easier than keeping on struggling, struggling, struggling." Kenneth, speaking about the men's hostel, reported that the rules were gentler now than the old days. (They used to wait until 11 o'clock to tell men that there would be no bed, and send them out into the night.) The language is less discriminatory and stigmatizing now. Fifteen years ago, the men in

---

[115] Culpitt, *Welfare and Citizenship*, 118.

the dorms were referred to as Transient Single Men or TSMs, where now all of the men are called "residents."

> We try to take the edge off that guy now ... Even if there are no beds you're not going to be out. Here is your supper ticket. Go eat and you'll be looked after.

The space offered by the provider often has an enabling structure, replacing an older scaffold of rules and constraints. People, especially ex-psychiatric patients, told Monique that they have approved the institutional nature of the hostel. They would say, "I messed up, I really need to be here for a little while because I need to stabilize." Structure gets people moving in the morning, gives them a schedule and a slate of activities.

"Family" Bonds, Social Support

There are aspects of the family in Street Aid. Patricia is intent on building "the trust relationship" with her street people. That means, you are not a "rat" and simply turn people into the police. Street Aid wants to help, not to bust people. (Sometimes the service providers provide alibis that will keep a client out of jail.) But, she advises, you must do counselling in depth for a number of reasons, one of which is that you must know their histories or you can be duped.

The helping spaces offer social support. The environment of help is not as artificial as in configurations A and B. There are designed features in the hostels that are quasi-familial or quasi-parental. The peer group arrangement is intended to evolve social skills and healing energies. The claim to being a family-substitute is not fanciful, for these are the places that will take you in even when your family does not want you. At the street ministry, Patricia affirms that "What you become down here is a family." They have put on weddings, birthday parties, funeral services — functions that women with babies, bag ladies, and "winos" cannot afford. So they put the event on, drive the couple through the city honking horns, take them to the Rose Garden, and send them back the pictures. Monique found that the young people in the hostel craved the support of staff and the peer group interaction. These interactions often provide "such parenting as they seem to get, or big sistering, or big brothering."

Funding and Staffing Shortages

Many service agencies are underfunded and short of staff to deal with increased demand. For example, the Family Mediation Service working out of the police station is so understaffed that they can barely cover the needs. There are too few holidays. The staff, being older, is more prone to becoming sick and burned out. More important for client service, counselling time becomes reduced and one-on-one services decline. Monique indicated that there are no resources for intensive treatment or intensive sustained referral (one-on-one with follow-up). Follow-up of any kind becomes rare. People with problems simply fall through the cracks. "There are a lot of people," Monique went on, "and so we really don't have the resources to do more than support and referral. It may take weeks and weeks before a successful referral is made. In the meantime, the clients may move out and the forward linkage to the other agency is broken. They are out of the helping loop."

Overworked and understaffed services often become more bu-reaucratic. Partly to cope with all the people at the Food Bank, limits have been set to how often people can go and what they can get, and the identification procedures are more thorough. Also lost are the proactive outreach and community services, as activities become more practical and reactive. Organizations are cramped for space — families are crowded into one room at a hostel or shelter and donated food is turned away because there is no space in which to store it.

Concluding Analysis

We are at an important juncture at this point. In the earlier configurations, low-income persons were regarded as a case to which this or that policy, rule, or referral applies. Or, as in configuration "A," the poor are construed as figures in a moral allegory. In both cases, they were assimilated to a powerful conditioning apparatus that wanted to reconfigure their subjectivi-ties to forms readable by the provider. Their own human situation was slighted, the knowledge only they could supply about their situation was screened out, and the resistive and transformative elements of their total situation were suppressed. They were consigned to a static position, reproducing the conditions of their domination.

In role "C," there is more learning from the poor and often a high degree of empathy into their situation. They are coming into view more as "poor people" than "paupers." Much of the help is neutral and supportive, especially of the need for relief from street and family troubles. Religious convictions are at play here, but they are neither imposed on the people to be helped nor used to allegorize their poverty. For example, Patricia and her husband's religion (fundamentalist Christian) helped redeem them from personal and family disorganization (she had been a runaway). It put remorse to work in a disciplined reconstruction of the couple's selves and enabled them to put the lessons of their early lives into the service of troubled youth.

In general, providers with the primary mode of needs responding were open to other modes; for example, they would join community initiatives on housing problems. And they are popular. Evidence suggests that people prefer services to be provided by local community agencies rather than state organizations — especially agencies that seem to them to be more related to them "either ethnically, culturally, religiously, locally or in respect of gender."[116]

I wish now to look at some problems of the needs responding configuration — its individualistic focus and the unplanned proliferation of services. I conclude with a vision of a fellowship presented by Jacob.

Individualistic Perspective

It would be unwise to take the individualistic, personalistic assumptions of Jacob and extend them to, say, social assistance recipients. When people lack what they need for a decent living, a personalist counsellor who does not address these rigid constraints on the poor offers uplift instead of upward mobility. Counselling of this sort, expressing the personal agency of the counsellor but no prospect of change for the client, becomes a kind of self-indulgence (as observed in configuration "A" as well).

---

[116] Ibid., 15.

Joan, an activist minister, senses the misplaced focus of this set of assumptions, which seems to look out of the wrong end of a pair of binoculars. "Most of our social services deal with people as individuals and don't help them to identify the fact that there's a social structure that's oppressing them. The food bank mentality deals with people as individuals: 'I'm going to help *you* so that you can take these groceries home and feed your family'." Mired in the apparent dysfunctions of *persons*, the helper begins to see the inadequate efforts at coping with hard circumstances as the *cause* of the fall into degradation and dependency.[117] This is the advanced version of the blame-the-victim perspective, to which the providers of the "C" configuration are prone. As Procacci has put it, "it is not poverty as the stigma of inequality that is combated, but pauperism understood as a cluster of behaviours, a carrier of difference."[118] "C" is still in part a variant of the anti-pauperism project, pauperism here understood as a cluster of deficits and situational stresses.

So what are the right emphases for the anti-individualistic critics of the "C" approach? Joan thinks we should attack the system that causes delays in the mailing of social assistance cheques and underpays people so much as to keep them poor. Organization people do this, Joan admits, but they are so overwhelmed with practical needs that they cannot make a systemic critique. (Joan and some other radical activists have the benefit of church support for their independent community stances.) Another system focus (as opposed to only coping with the personal results of low funding) would be to push for the harmonization of benefits with a more generous and sustaining community standard.

The needs responders' personal inadequacy approach aligns it in its core assumption with most of the social services field (especially "A" and "B"). There is such a systemic blindness in the field to structural constraints operating beyond the individual-situational level that radical activists end up mistrusting *any* program that aims to develop the "human capital" of low-income people. As the anti-poverty activist Joseph puts it, "They need to be trained, they need to be made better people through social workers sitting

---

[117] Miller, "Community development," 226.

[118] Procacci, "Social economy," 164.

down with them and showing them the error of their ways." The
basic problem, for Joseph, is that there are not enough decent-paying jobs for people and, until that is corrected, all the training and
help is misguided.[119] His conclusion seems exaggerated until you
understand his attitude as an antipathy and distrust at the whole
vast enterprise of fixing, counselling, motivating and identifying the
poor *individual*; i.e., the "pauper."

Over-servicing: The Proliferation of Needs Responders

   Liberal capitalist society in general, and the social services field
in particular, by ignoring the root causes (and solutions) of poverty
and the inequality bred by its routine structures and practices, open
a Pandora's box of symptomatic treatments of poverty. To configure
low-income persons as a bundle of needs, or deficits, or problems — to which one's self or organization responds — is to set in
motion a vast engine of human endeavour. Needs assessments,
mission statements, formation of groups, filling out of grant appli-
cations, establishment of jobs and careers — all this specialized,
focused effort has a vested interest in the formulation and treatment
of poverty as a set of needs. At the organizational level, there is no
initial funding if you cannot identify a need and no continuing
support if you cease responding to that need. The danger is,
especially in the absence of genuine dialogue with low-income
people, that the organization assesses needs which *it* is capable of
meeting. Social service and social workers then become guardians
of these services, underlying the fact that providers have a deep
self-interest in modes of giving.[120] At the collegial and individual
levels, needs responding can become the basis of a satisfying career
and a means of living an ethical and purposeful life with others.

   An important question for a study that takes the standpoint of
the poor is: does the fragmentary, poorly coordinated multiplication
of individual services focusing on individual clients diminish the
well-being of recipients? Yes, according to the activist Joan. Her
people often cannot come to community functions because they

---

[119] This assessment is arguable in those cases where there is a skills mismatch between
workers and job vacancies. Training would be helpful here.

[120] Culpitt, *Welfare and Citizenship*, 67.

are too busy being serviced by service providers. "Everything from health inspectors to health nurses to F&CS [Family and Community Services] workers to welfare workers to, you know, you name it and somebody had made an appointment with somebody for some kind of social service." When someone is in crisis, she continues, and there are "five presenting issues and they're being dealt with by five different agencies in five different ways, very often things undermine each other." An example follows. Let us say that an agency or worker wants to send a person to school for upgrading. but Welfare is not giving enough financial help. The person cannot get a loan from this other agency, nor can she get sufficient child care to go back to school. As a result, the official in the original organization says (in Joan's words), "'Well, obviously, this person is not trying very hard to upgrade themself,' and so they cut back on the support in terms of going back to school." She has demonstrated that there are real dysfunctions for the low-income person stemming from uncoordinated services.

How can you coordinate needs in a way that does not simply feed the social service careers of the planners and unleash turf wars among providers? The community-minded providers suggest that we must have a community vantage point on needs that forces us to ask holistic questions. One of the community voices (which will have their say in the next chapter) is Joanne's, whose base is a clinic on abused women. Given that low-income people have so many needs, she asked the following: Is the meeting of these needs being coordinated? Are gaps in service being identified? We must, at least conceptually, pull away from the individual trees to get a glimpse of the forest.

It must be constantly kept in mind, however, that there are limits to the degree of success that social workers and other service providers can expect and be held accountable for. Part of the "forest" of advantage and disadvantage are patterns of racism, gender discrimination, and accumulated market rejection and ex- ploitation of poor people. These require deep-rooted changes in the political economy. When we consider the awesome require- ments for transformation of the society, social workers should not be made to feel guilty if they are not up to *that* task: how could they be? Similarly, planners like Joanne would be wise not to show excessive hubris about the potential for community intelligence to smooth out entrenched inequalities.[121]

A Helper's Vision

It is difficult to be unmoved by Jacob's honesty about his unfulfillment and personal need. His helping is his art. "It's a little bit like art or music, or some trade or skill that you can learn, that you don't have to be born with. You enjoy the positive characteristics of the people you work with." At the end of the interview, his vision expands to present his helping community as a kind of fecund artistic achievement:

> Every single individual is different, and every single individual has something to offer ... then you work with that individual. The word "work" is not the right word, because you fellowship, and you associate, and you create, and you do it together. It's almost like an expanding friendship.

He imagines people looking at his Skid Row rehab centre and figuring that there are a "bunch of drunks flopped all over the place. If they could only know. How would they ever imagine there's so much to go on in here? I mean there are so many things to do."

This is an impressive, even inspiring, vision of a caring community — notwithstanding all the earlier reservations about the boundary-crossing prerogatives of empathy. But for others, caring should infuse the whole community which should include the poor on a basis of justice not empathy. The sense of personal agency of the provider helping the personal agency of the wounded to come to its feet is, it must be said, a severely limited model. The community-minded and anti-poverty workers and activists make the larger claim that community and societal agency is the proper transformative force to awaken and channel — not the realm of persons and helpers.

---

[121] Ibid., 190.

6

"D": Community Developing

*T*here were service providers who thought that the way to provide for low-income people was to fortify their place and entitlements in neighbourhoods and community. They were less interested in the crafting of humane spaces to meet personal needs than in breaking up the ghettos the poor were made to live in. Above all, the aim was to include the disenfranchised in normal community processes — living in decent housing, doing self-sustaining work, entering in civic life. Though there were many providers who had community-oriented ideas, five made it a central focus of their efforts. These included two ministers working in poor communities in the city, a priest committed to social justice projects, and two community workers in the fields of housing and wife abuse.

Self-presentation

The "D" configuring mode has anti-*poverty* as its project, not anti-pauperism. It disassociates itself entirely from the socialization of paupers into the moral project of order, which preoccupy many providers of "A," "B," or "C" configuring modes. They want to distinguish their efforts from all those who want to infuse the poor with a normalizing discipline. Donzelot calls this group the "tutelary complex":

> Even in areas of social life that remained relatively free of carceral discipline — e.g., the family and community — there developed a corresponding formation of normalising discipline, which Donzelot terms the "tutelary complex." This comprises the growing "swarm" of social workers, benefits officers, psychiatrists, educators, and so forth who intervene in the plight of, for example, the deprived child and family, and today constitute the modern welfare state.[122]

---

[122] Hewitt, *Welfare, Ideology and Need*, 161-162.

Both the tutelary group and the community providers in the sample want the poor to be integrated into society, but in a crucially different way. The former group want the poor to be socialized into a moral order that will continue to be unequal and whose maladjusted elements will be addressed individualistically and therapeutically. The "D" (and "E") providers want the poor to be integrated into a community (and society) which is starting to assume collective agency, especially as it transforms its structures and practices to accommodate the healthy personal agents who were once excluded and impoverished.

Poverty is a far vaster pageant than pauperism; those who grapple with it are noticing larger outlines of the phenomenon, not the psychological details. We see here a perceptual and analytical focus that is more macrosocial. In this configuration, empathy is not a personally fulfilling end in itself, but rather a means of gathering social knowledge for a vast project of inclusion of low-income people into the community. People are seen as social subjects and citizens, whose community lives and social identities suffer from lack of inclusion and resources.

Conception of the Low-income Subject

The poor are constructed and subjectified here as active participants in the process of community. These are not abstract, incomplete subjects whose deficits are to be identified and divided among helpers in a project of tutelage. Low-income people have remedial work to do in education and skill-building, granted, but they "also must be implicated in the order into which they are to be integrated."[123] The tutelage system sets a professional class to work on a project of normalization of a class of low-income people, all of which is an exercise in class domination by gatekeepers and experts in "symbolic capital." The community providers here want to reconstitute the normal processes of community so that they reduce the class differentiation and isolation of the poor. The stigma of difference, which the anti-pauperists see as the eradicable cause of poverty, is here seen as the *result* of the segregation of poor people

---

[123] Procacci, "Social economy," 166.

in the community. It is that segregation which is the pathology, not the attributes of the poor.

The low-income person constructed here is a politically responsible subject who can enter civic life and politics. The poor should be present in the neighbourhoods of the city and have an opportunity to participate in the security that property confers. Lower-income people must be wrenched free from their special niches in segregated neighbourhoods and from the abstract official spaces and designs of the conventional government planner.

The earlier role configurations dealt with micro-practices, whereas the present configuration supports meso-practices, aimed at developing community. (Role "E," explored in the next chapter, is committed to "macro-practices."[124]) The configurative practices of Role "D" are two: delegitimizing and opposing community barriers, and sustaining positive community ties with and among low-income people.

Delegitimizing and Opposing Community Obstacles to Equal Participation

A major originating cause of poverty, according to the community providers, is the community's ejection of the poor from its normal round of life. "You're looking at people," according to Donald, a priest involved in the community, "who are excluded and who are aware that they are excluded, who know that they are being systematically excluded." From this primal exclusion flows the ills suffered by the poor (drugs, crime, apathy, etc.), which are their reactive formations. The "D" configuration brings us into a sociological sensibility adopted by lay actors (though some are sociologically educated). The psychology of persons becomes less deep and elaborated, partly due to an aversion to psychological "explanations" of poverty which blame the poor. Indeed there is a contrary tendency (even stronger in "E") towards methodological holism, where collectivities such as "community," "society," "middle class," and so on, are given the attributes of self-conscious agents (as in "the society rejects," "the middle class has contempt, etc."). The

---

[124] Saldov, "Unemployment," 215.

social psychology adopted tends to be action-oriented and prag-
matic. The poor are seen, like other humans, as inherently active,
but whose agency is circumscribed by barriers not of their own
making. (As Colleen, who is in a public housing ministry, stated: "I
guess the myth that bothers me the most is the fault one. You must
have done something to deserve it.")

Contextual Realism: Webs of Constraint

The informants in this role configuration are very informative on
the complex interactions of low-income persons with the various
obstructive circumstances that exclude them from community life.
Joanne calls them the "strong barriers that people face." Before
depicting these barriers (housing, lack of money, bureaucratic and
charity practices, work disincentives), it would help to examine the
contextual realism of these providers and their implicit conception
of societal webs.

The community developer's sensibility is marked by contextual
realism, which refuses to see problems in isolation. The thread of
one problem is followed until it finally reveals its attachments to a
complex webbing of environmental, interpersonal and economic
contingencies. An example would be poor housing, a major
destabilizer of low-income people's lives. As Doris, the family
consultant with the police, put it: "We have clients, every time they
turn around it sounds like the landlord is threatening to evict … It's
just so unstable, as one more part of their life that's unstable." The
community analyst sees housing instability as connected to a web
of economic insufficiency. Chris's analysis is a case in point, where
housing instability branches out to a conception of a whole class
structure:

> If you've got money, you've got power. It's that simple. And you
> would have a lease or you would able to afford a lawyer or you'd
> be educated enough, even if you didn't know the law, to realize
> you were being taken.

Without money, you must rely on Legal Aid or advocacy services
which are hard to find. So the problems form a web. To be
enfranchised into the community, poor people must have jobs as
well as housing. Chris, refusing to abstract problems from their
context, illuminates one of the connecting strands of the web: "Most
people want jobs. It's interrelated; you can't isolate housing from

unemployment. I mean it's the same kind of issue." If one adds a decent job to the minimum of decent house, one has a path to self-sufficiency. (It is partly to the absence of jobs and housing, one could fairly say, that a veritable industry of help providers owes its living.)

This branching, reticular view of, say, housing problems is extended outward spatially. The forces bearing on the local places where low-income people live their lives are increasingly global. Cities, and the financing of the development within them, are exposed to a world capitalist market. The commercialization of real estate (and much of city space) converts real places into abstract spaces, for both the elites that profit and the poor that are displaced. Capitalist elites now see their markets and field of operations as global and are less attentive to the local needs of the cities they do business in. As the other side of the same process, the poor that are priced out of commercial real estate can be seen as ejected from place and forced to inhabit the policy space of subsidized housing. It is *place,* especially for people who are not market players, that the "C" providers want to defend against the abstracting economic forces that threaten it. "Place" means the wherewithal for commu- nity living — good affordable housing, proximity to shops and services, friendly ties with neighbours, and occasions for citizen action.

There is a regional bearing as well. Faced with housing and economic insufficiencies, poor people leave smaller towns for London and, when they do not get what they need here, go on to Toronto. "So the province's problems, homeless problems, collect in Toronto," according to Chris. He faults communities for simply disowning their poor, whether by tight-fisted policies or obstacles to integration, hoping that they will simply head down the road to more accommodating cities. He thinks that you cannot solve Toronto's problems unless you solve local problems. Community- oriented providers oppose the public choice notion that people's individualistic choices must govern their community choices and patterns. Communities must entitle the poor with the "ballast" of citizenship — materialized in homes and jobs — not just leave them unanchored to float to the biggest city or more adequate welfare jurisdiction. The idea of moving the poor around has already taken bizarre twists — an apartment owner in Sarnia bid for some of

Alberta's poor to live in his subsidized units. Moving more by compulsion than choice, the poor are in danger of being shunted around like a modern market version of the indentured worker auctions of pre-Confederation times.

The community providers want to convert a planless, market-like transmission belt of poor people (based on a public choice model of agency) to a network of socially responsible, integrating communities which are consciously altering their own normal processes to include the marginalized (based on a model of *community* agency). To make a relatively affluent city conscious about and responsible for its poor is an uphill battle, Chris attests:

> So if there are enough alternatives here in the community that we can keep our people, then that's what we need to do. And that's been quite a thing to sell in London.

Why is the idea "hard to sell"? A major factor is the community's apparent ignorance of (or resistance to) the poverty in its midst. London projects an affluent self-image, from which low-income people are screened out. Media surveys of Londoners exclude the topic, and a major publication on poverty by the United Way received little general publicity or circulation. Expensive transportation keeps many of the poor from coming downtown, and there are exclusionary practices operating in neighbourhoods. When these filters are operating, there is a mistaken impression of the middle-class homogeneity of Londoners which covers up the growing gap between rich and poor. Joanne, trying to fathom the blinkered mind of affluent London, said, "we're trying not to acknowledge that too clearly, or too vocally, and not to advocate on behalf of those who need help ... We have been slow to listen to those who are not as privileged." This presents one of the mandates of the "C" provider — educating the community about low-income people, and why and how the community must exercise its social responsibilities to them.

But it is critical to enlist *low-income people themselves* in this educational and political project. Community-based action wants to ensure that those who suffer disadvantage in the community have a voice to communicate their situation and make effective demands on those who dominate them. The help they receive must empower them to gain a measure of control over their situation — whether it be housing, legal advice, education, or whatever. The "C" providers are keenly aware of the disempowering aspects of the usual modes of helping. As Donnison writes,

> Whatever it may be, if it is provided at the behest and under the control of others — the professionals, the politicians, the philanthropists — we may be sure that it will work in ways which ultimately reinforce the victims' exclusion, humiliation and sense of powerlessness.[125]

Community action aims to redirect that downward flow of power so that it is channelled horizontally, among community groups and enabling specialists, and upward, as the voice of the poor ascends with its demands.

Housing Barriers

Ghettoizing the Poor

The community sensibility of the providers was repelled by the segregation of poor people in obvious public housing ghettos. Jacob found them to be "awful places" where people were "all junked together." "We should find them places," he added, "where they're not obvious." As a case in point, we have the north London public housing project where Colleen is chaplain. This townhouse complex was built in the middle of a field. Gradually middle-class homeowners to the west and very affluent homeowners to the east moved into the area. Now the poor are completely segregated from but visible to the non-poor community around them. As Colleen expresses it: "We're isolated, we're discriminated against. It's a hunk of apartheid in northwest London. We're truly set apart here."

The public housing residents feel the prejudiced attitudes of merchants in the mall, and they know that the children of the better-off are told not to play in the homes of poor friends. As a result, the inhabitants feel shame at even admitting where they live.

Market Forces against the Poor

Market forces constantly erect barriers to the poor's integration into permanent, affordable housing — in the central city, especially. There is very little centrally-located land available for low-income people. There are co-operatives, some pockets of non-profit hous-

---

[125] Donnison, "Social policy," 218-219.

ing, and a number of apartments one can secure through maintenance work, but for the most part development is geared to the
private developer and home-owner. "Why are the low-cost inner-
city housing places being destroyed," Joanne asked, "and being
replaced by large and expensive condominiums?" She is calling to
account the whole political process of assenting to market forces
which has made change faceless and ungraspable. Who controls
this process and why has it become so expensive to provide social
housing? The capitalist dynamic of adding value to real estate
actually prices the poor, and policy-makers, out of realistic housing
options. Much of the dwindling stock of housing that is available
is treated by unscrupulous speculators as sources of quick profit,
giving the tenants little protection against their units being sold and
renovated into unaffordability. As well, neglectful owners and
exploitative landlords often let their rooming houses run down
often with the long-term aim of selling when the area's real estate
values increase.

Apart from the economic filters of high rents and the requirement
of first and last month's rent, there is active discrimination against
low-income persons in the housing market (as was mentioned in
Chapter 2). Landlords often contract out to apartment rental services, which are instructed to screen out unaffluent single parents
and the unemployed. The unemployed, lacking money coming in,
are definitely screened out by landlords. But the stigmatization
extends much more widely, according to Chris: "People are more
willing to rent to a student ... than they are to an ex-psychiatric
patient or someone who is just plain poor, who doesn't present too
well, who is maybe a little shabby."

The active discrimination extends into the suburbs as well, who
are less community-minded now. Suburbanites feel encroached
upon by unfamiliar people and what they feel are excessive tax
demands to pay for the problems of others. There is more mistrust
and guardedness regarding policies favouring the disadvantaged.[126]
People in suburbs pay more for housing now and have longer
commuting times to work — which adds to their sense of individualism. They are likely to be resistant to, say, the halfway or group

---

[126] Wolfe, *Whose Keeper?*, 68.

homes for the mentally disabled and juvenile delinquents and tend to tar all public policy housing initiatives with the same brush. Chris finds that "we all get lumped together with some of the different kinds of group homes and people don't get beyond 'group home' ... When you try to talk to them about non-profit housing it's really an alien concept to them. So it takes a lot of selling."

What is Needed

Given these filters and barriers, what do the community workers recommend? They want an overall plan for integrating low-income people throughout the city. Ideally, in all official plans for every new subdivision or planning district, there would be a variety of housing types, including those accommodating lower-income people — social housing, non-profits, group homes, co-operatives. This would be permanent and affordable housing, of good quality, and well dispersed in the community so as to avoid stigma.

Also needed is centrally located housing for low-income people. They need accessibility to a plaza or downtown to get cheaply to stores and services. Phones and transportation are expensive. "And if you've got two or three kids to lug on a bus," Chris said, "you don't want to be too far away from a store." As well, lower-income individuals often rely more on reciprocal ties and mutual aid among kin relations than middle-class people.[127] Contiguity of such networks, therefore, is more important to lower-class persons; if they are not near, transportation subsidies are appropriate. Such vulnerable groups as refugees and immigrants, battered women, and youth need central housing even more in order to get to required services. Community outreach workers offer advocacy under the housing registry downtown to help connect poor people with convenient living spaces.

The politicians have no policy on affordable housing, such as looking into, for instance, where to put non-profit or social housing in the central city or in new housing areas. Politicians tend to go along with the developers and try not to rile the suburbanites with their "Not in my backyard" attitudes. Chris's suggestion is to modify bylaws to increase neighbourhood densities, and especially to

---

[127] Ibid., 57.

encourage people to "rehab" places so as to increase the available number of rooms. We need to make room for the marginalized in the mainstream neighbourhoods of the city.

Uncommunal Social Services and Charities

The community-minded providers are not always agreed on a concrete vision of the good community, but their images of anti-community are sharp and affecting. Colleen was approached by a woman who needed food and had missed a deadline for a food basket from a church. She could not bring herself to go to a well-known religious charity. Colleen offered to accompany her and she still declined; so she went ahead and arranged for a food hamper on the woman's behalf. The portrait by Colleen of the atomizing conditions at that charity, especially given the season, was graphic:

> I've been there and I come away appalled and just upset and say there is no way in North America that people should have to go through this. Lines of people not looking at each other; everyone averts lifting their eyes in case they recognize anyone that's there. Sometimes the TV cameras come in so that there is this wonderful story of Christmas with the Christian Army. Everybody has got these little handfuls of paper, cause if you're missing one of the papers they will turn you down; you need to come back the next day with the rest of the papers. It's usually cold; you're outside because the queue is in the building and out. There's no coffee provided. It's the least thing that resembles Christmas that I've ever seen.

This is extremely offensive to the community role configuration: the charity plucks people out of dignified community and arranges them in serial formation for the various uses of the organization. At least for a time, it extinguishes the low-income person's social identity.

One of the most powerful impulses felt by people, rich and poor, is to make a living doing self-reliant work. This desire to contribute to family and society is like a strong cohesive current of energy between individuals and society. Colleen sees this desire in its frustrated form among Central American immigrants who lose their profession in the struggle simply to survive:

> There is great grieving over loss of profession ... that can lead to alcoholism. They can smile at me and tell me, "It's great to be in Canada, and my children will be free." But you scratch just a little below the surface and there is grieving ... But there is a firm

resolve on their part that they will be one-generation poverty and
their kids will go on to university.

She tries to feel the pain of being a teacher in El Salvador who
cannot even find a job selling hot dogs.

Against the strong integrating force of the pursuit of work, the
bureaucratic systems erect disincentives for poor people who are
on benefits.This enrages the community sensibility of the providers.
Before the levels of allowable earnings recently increased somewhat, if a child got a paper route, the income of his family on social
assistance dropped. Women on family benefits are afraid to get even
part-time work because they will lose extended medical coverage
for their children. When a person on benefits finds a job, rent
subsidies immediately fall away, complicating the jump to the work
force. Colleen, among others, thought that rent subsidies should be
phased out more gradually as people integrate into working life.
Note the sharp difference between this vantage point and the
abstract bureaucratic one. The location here is people's needs in
their actual lives in community.

Effects of Poverty: Crime and Escapism

It is thought, in this role configuration, that much crime is a
desperate recourse to which people are driven when they are
locked out of decent housing and jobs. When people are desperate,
they work for unreported income in the informal economy, they
do prostitution on the side, and they do break-and-enters. Chris
notes, "You get all the ripple effect of these kinds of thing when
times get rough. [With] the jobs that people get, you steal bicycles,
get $200 easy for a bicycle. That's how they get it." Crime is a means
of survival.

As well, poor people engage in escapist behaviour, such as
abusing drugs. "The greatest plague," according to Colleen, "is the
abuse of drugs; i.e., alcohol, cigarettes, street drugs, prescribed
drugs." These are the ways to dull the pain of lowered self-esteem,
anger, depression and the feeling of being discriminated against.
The conviction of the community configuration is not that the poor
are weak, but weakened.

Learning and Supporting Community with and among Low-income People

The service providers have depicted a pattern of community repulsions and exclusions of those who are poor, so it is not surprising that their policy suggestions are pointed to improving access to resources and making it easier for people to integrate into a normal working life. They want to equalize welfare benefits of all kinds and bring them to a level that is demonstrably adequate for community needs. As was mentioned, they bridle at the discriminatory benefit levels of the so-called deserving and undeserving poor because they introduce bureaucratic-moralistic restrictions to meeting real-world needs out in the community. Similarly, in the year or so of a person getting established in a job, they support phasing out shelter allowances slowly. In more general terms, what is their concept and practice of developing community?

Being with, and Learning from, Low-income People

The first principle is to go where low-income people live and express solidarity with them as an equal. The idea is not so much to "help" them as to "work with" them. Equipped with a vision of people as creative human agents whose powers are partially stifled by the obstacles of poverty, the provider tends to be resistant to the feelings of disrespect and condescension that some other providers have. Flaws are seen as, in large part, the effect of community rejection rather than the stigmatizing attributes attached to individuals.

The initial contact with low-income people, for the chaplain and activist minister, was going door to door in the public housing community and introducing herself in a low-key manner. In a reversal of more conservative forms of service provision, the provider must gain the trust of the people. The books and pencils (which the agency people use to make their reports) are put away, for there is no gathering of data for reports that assess or monitor eligibility. Colleen visits them in their homes, listening, establishing rapport and gaining trust. The message is that we are interested in you as members of the community, not just as cases or numbers or grist for our bureaucratic mill.

Relationships are constructed more freely, unrestrained by the usual boundaries between professional and client. Power relations between community developer and low-income people are more equitable, indeed at first seem to give more power to the latter. The poor are free to refuse to construct themselves as members of community. So they can stay home when meetings are held, can refuse to participate in community ventures, and can simply withhold their support. From the service provider's vantage point, the poor are more constituency than clientele. Their attendance at meetings and support of initiatives validate the provider's personal commitment and community methodology. (For the minister-providers in this study, it probably had the added merit of making people aware of the church, but this was never stated as an explicit aim. There is a larger design here, however. The liberal Protestant denominations are not conceding lower-income people to the recruiting efforts of the fundamentalist churches.)

Enormous emphasis is placed on patient, empathetic learning from low-income people. There is an almost visceral resistance to generalizations about types or characteristics of "the poor." The route to knowledge is ethnographic: to have been with the poor, to have experienced what they are experiencing. For instance, Colleen took a course in addiction that she had been recommending to people. Providers will tell of the poverty they themselves have known or the experiential education they have had. Joan took a course in urban analysis which required her to:

> go out and live on the streets of Toronto for three days and three nights with no money — so that I could really have the experience of powerlessness. And I think that exposure to powerlessness certainly shaped my perspective on what happens to people when they're poor and what happens to them when they have to deal with social service agencies that want to, "help them." I got a totally different perspective on the helping agencies when you're on the street and have to accept charity from people. It's a really humiliating experience.

She was in a ministry for two years in a Nova Scotia fishing village with high unemployment, then with impoverished Mexican Mennonite tobacco pickers in Elgin country, Ontario.

The community provider's mode of learning often takes the form of informal interviews on needs and service gaps — with the difference that it projects outward to facilitate rehabilitative and social interchanges. The data-gathering is aimed to acquire knowledge that is detailed and socially constructive, as opposed to stereotyped, bureaucratic, or moralistic. Human details are of absorbing interest not as voyeuristic invasions of privacy or clinical data on their own account, but rather as socio-psychological and cultural elements of the necessarily subtle transformations and inclusions that can lead low-income people out of their situations.

The providers show intense admiration for the resourcefulness and determination of low-income people who struggle against the odds. Contrary to stereotype, Colleen finds many of the homes in the complex quite clean and tidy: "If anything there is an overre-action: 'we may be poor but we won't be dirty'." Low-income mothers are highly regarded for the disciplined way they manage their small amounts of money. This is an impressive achievement particularly in view of the injuries to self-esteem inflicted by poverty. As Joan said with passion:

> If a woman is still trying to provide for her children after five years of being told she's a failure each month, you know, what kind of inner stamina does she have to keep on coping?

She claimed that she herself would be "bloody dysfunctional" under conditions of poverty which makes one feel isolated and worthless. For her part, Colleen admits that there is the anger, drugs, and defeatism of some, but that is only half of it. "The other half is that I see extra strength that I stand in awe of." Despite these strikes against people, they try so hard to succeed. This "great strength in people and how they're coping in getting ahead" is what keeps her from burning out.

Fortifying Their Community Connections

It is vital that low-income people overcome their sense of isolation in their homes and "apartheid" community. The provider tries to rekindle in demoralized people some social hope and confidence. The aim is to draw them to real world involvements and community satisfactions and away from the inner-world es-capes in drugs. Out of the community linkages fostered and strengthened by providers, a community politics may emerge. Colleen found "nuclear" mutual aid networks in the complex: "clusters of sharing in here ... geographical clusters where clothes get switched around and babysitting gets done for no money, and that kind of 'We have to help each other because the masks of the middle class are gone'." This same kind of community formation is done at the Soup Kitchen, with its tolerant attitude and regular availability for people to meet.

Examples of community gathering points would be courses on addiction, woman's time out, parenting skill classes, etc. But providers try to amplify the scope of community organization beyond the neighbourhood setting. Given the token funding and attention given to the community by macro-politics, Chris particularly emphasized the need for community-based advocacy groups. What is needed is intense group involvement and education — fostering community awareness, trying to find housing for vulnerable groups, educating the social justice groups in the churches, housing refugees. In this vein, the United Church runs a coffee house for Chris's low-income seekers of housing. Some of the church people are housing refugees and youth. Chris was heartened by these ventures: "I don't think you can underestimate the power of the voluntary sector or the citizen once they are aware." He thought that the middle class, now feeling the bite of unemployment, are starting to ask the right questions.

Concluding Analysis

The community empowerment movement is disdainful of many national policies that try to improve the economic situation of depressed communities by giving incentives to large corporations to invest, or by setting up training programs for people to acquire the skills to move elsewhere. These large-scale programs reduce the local community to either passive participants or constituents exercising veto power. By contrast, local initiatives are proactive economic and servicing ventures that incite energetic commitments in the community. Implicit also in the community empowerment model is a rejection of the purely individualistic ethos of the marketplace. Between national programs and the marketplace stands a host of possibilities for development and welfare in the community.

The Romance of Community

Is a subtle kind of exchange being revealed in these accounts? What are the providers getting out of their community-based action?

In this configuration providers' gifts of time and personal sacrifice
are not immediately or conventionally rewarded, but that is not the
point. Through their own personal agency, they are helping to make
a group that will be a collective agent in a wider field of endeavour.
In that wider field, the provider's personal ideals can be enacted,
thus raising self-esteem and self-efficacy. More generally, the
provider will have found a social setting where the corruptions of
individual market society will be transcended. In short, therre is a
utopian strain in the community-minded who want to see behind
the empirical reality of the groups they help create an image of the
good society they have long been seeking.

That there may be a mythic or fictive element in the community
discerned by the community provider is attested to by the sheer
uncommunal hodge-podge of people and situations that form
public housing. This is not like a suburb where the inhabitants have
moved in voluntarily, being in some genereal affinity with the types
of people that will be their neighbours. Public housing have
conglomerations of people who feel that they have been dumped
there, or are biding time through a transitional phase, or are
planning ways to get out. The community impulses fostered there
are, of course, all the more vital — but Colleen's imaging of the
poor in her public housing project is revealing:

> Liberation theology that came out of Central America is wonderful.
> This is a base community. We have a Bible study group on Friday
> mornings that is like the ones used in Central America where we
> sing verses from the scripture, then the poor speak to it. It's not
> religion coming from the top down. It's religion coming from faith,
> coming from the hearts of the poor.

What does she contrast this base community with? The hierarchical
church whose compromises have corrupted it.

> The churches as institutions are hierarchical, are controlling of a lot
> of money and privilege, and I don't see them wanting to change
> very much ... I think the institutionalized church is dying. Maybe it
> should die sooner than later. Hopefully cluster groups of Christianity
> will spring up, where persons can stand in solidarity.

We can perhaps see now the hoped-for reward for the provider in
the romantic view of community — it is the finding of goodness in
a corrupted world. In placing herself in and identifying with a
marginal community (which the provider has helped constitute),
she can participate in a more ideal, poorer church animated by a

socially responsible, more innocent faith. This prophetic community, composed of involuntary and voluntary poor (i.e., the helper), embodies a morality which is superior (by virtue of being poor) to the affluent. "There is now a real danger," Donnison writes, "that the old romanticism about the state will be succeeded by new romanticisms about communities and markets."[128]

Assessment of Community-Based Approaches

Community-based approaches to meeting the needs of the disadvantaged are immensely important. The service providers and activists who committed themselves to this approach are deservedly proud of their ability to listen to people within their living contexts and to provide services within, or with an awareness of, these contexts. People pick up a sense of optimism about the potentialities of the community at hand and "tested leaders … may reappear at an important time."[129]

Still, reservations should be expressed. The providers — sensing that they are empowering people, and being themselves empowered and esteemed in the process — tend to promote community-based services as *the* answer to the shortcomings of conventional public, or private, services. The community partisans find the public official too authoritarian and the private entrepreneur too mercenary and profit-driven. But cannot the service delivery to individuals by public officials and private sector be made more responsive and "user-friendly"?[130] If so, perhaps people would prefer these conventional services to the time-intensive involvements offered in community-based services.

Community-based groups have their drawbacks. Single-purpose groups stick to their function and tend not to train and mobilize people for other work. Having committed to each other over years of meetings, people develop strong personal bonds and a home-grown power structure. Having become habituated to the familiar system, people are often unreceptive to new ideas or types of people. As well, the *sanctions* against rule breakers, lacking a

---

[128] Donnison, "Social policy," 204.

[129] Miller, "Poverty and respect," 223.

[130] Donnison, "Social policy," 208.

foundation in bureaucratic authority structure, can turn out to be harsh and socially rejecting.[131] A further vulnerability is that failure of a program or a venture can lead to community disillusionment and an increase in cynicism and fatalism.

The critique of the welfare rights paradigm made by Culpitt that there is an implicit anarchism "about any obligation beyond that owed to the community, tribe, group, family or network of similarity"[132] might be applied to the localism behind the proliferating community-based approaches. Do they widen or narrow the scope of mutual obligation and responsibility we should have for our fellow citizens? These approaches do improve local parts of the society, but their priority is the particular job they have taken on, not the economic and political forces shaping the exclusion of the disadvantaged. Not only are some local approaches non-responsive to the general problem of including the deprived in the mainstream of society, they may actually (in Donnison's words) "reinforce their exclusion and the problems of other neighbourhoods and institutions to which the excluded then have to resort."[133]

So localism can empower, selectively, but beyond its circle may curtail the widening of involvements and empowerments. Community activists must attend to macro-social and macro-economic policies, institutions, and funding needed to expand the empowering effect of worthwhile local programs.[134] Localities cannot go it alone. Alliances between state and community organizations may improve the chances that individual empowerment and community empowerment may converge, all the while addressing the requisite large scale in which problems of disadvantage have their origin.

---

[131] Ibid., (209) is generally good on the negative side of community-based approaches.

[132] Culpitt, *Welfare and Citizenship*, 22.

[133] Donnison, "Social policy," 210.

[134] Miller, "Poverty and respect," 223.

7

"E": Anti-poverty Activating

*T*he last role configuration, anti-poverty activating, takes as its field of organization and critique those domains just beyond the reach of the community providers — including municipal, provincial and federal institutions and politics. While a number of the providers configure the disadvantaged within both a community and anti-poverty mode, those who emphasize the latter involve themselves in action and critique against poverty (not pauperism), seen as a symptom of a system of inequality. Poverty is something produced in the markets, offices, schools and legislatures of the normal political economy. To "help" the poor, we must combine our efforts to protest against and change the present system which produces poverty.

How are low-income people altercast or viewed? The poor are seen as active but in chains. They are not deficit-ridden dependents or clients who need help, but whole people who are ensnared by economic obstacles and state control apparatuses. As Joseph, the anti-poverty activist, put it, "we've sought to mobilize people to rely on their own strength to actually go out and confront the powers that be." These powers are moving fundamental macro-"levers" that are shunting masses of people into disadvantage. A sense of the scope of the "powers that be" is conveyed by John Clarke, an influential anti-poverty figure in Ontario: "a vast transfer of workers into the low wage ghetto has been compounded by over a million people in Ontario being now forced to live on welfare ... at the mercy of a system of punitive, sub-poverty handouts."[135]

The self-presentation is not as a special professional group, or elite, or member of an organization. Rather, the activist appears as an ally of the poor, joining with them to pressure society to be mindful of its responsibilities to provide a decent living for all its

---

[135] Clarke, "Ontario's social movements," 213.

members. "Society" here is seen as dominated by oppressive powers of state and class who are committed to the imposition of a corporate agenda. To the more socialist activists, society is, potentially, a working coalition of popular movements and labour movements which are imbued with collective agency and purpose. As in "C," the activist needs to establish credibility with the low-income people he or she wishes to organize, thus reversing the usual validating direction of configurations "A," "B," and "C." The activist/critic tries to earn the trust of low-income people and establishes similar expectations for them as they become involved.

Radical and Reformist

To contextualize the radical and reformist variants of the anti-poverty perspective, we need to recall the Foucauldian perspective introduced earlier. The anxious bourgeoisie began to defend itself against the "indiscipline, the asocial autonomy, of the pauperized urban masses"[136] by setting in motion a vast project of incorporating the working class into the body politic. The conservative-authoritarian wing of this socialization project was exemplified in configurations "A" and "B." In this "vector of bourgeois class struggle ... the encounter between liberalism and socialism"[137] is very important. In the anti-poverty perspective in this study, the encounter is between moderate and radical positions.

The reformist or moderate position wants to call the political community to a sense of its proper social responsibility to reduce the inequality of opportunity and condition that produces poverty for so many of its citizens. So there is a thorough debunking of the unprogressive tax system, the governmental focus on fighting the deficit and inflation, and the lowering standards of social programs, wages, and working conditions promoted by free trade. The remedies are defensive strategies to bolster government programs and workers' protections encoded in law and union contracts. There is an emphasis on social integration of all citizens within a solidaristic, social democratic state. The reformists feel that broad-based

---

[136] Gordon, "Governmental Rationality," 31.
[137] Ibid.

alliances of the poor with many groups and classes would serve their interests. Through teaching, speaking out, helping to organize programs which include the disadvantaged in an active role, the reformist works for a humane society.

The radical approach is to establish solidarity with the poor in order to organize with them a collective resistance to the societal forces that produce poverty. What is demanded is, first, a policy of full employment — with jobs that allow people to make a decent living and have a say in their workplace. Until that time is reached, the radical defends welfare state programs which give people the wherewithal to survive by citizens' right. To attain full employment involves a defeat of the corporate agenda, whose mobile capital investment patterns play off one work-force against another to pursue the cheapest wages. Second, through confrontational actions, lobbying and mobilizing, the radical aims in the long run to undermine the capitalist system and to replace it with a socialist agenda that places workers' interests in the forefront of societal development.

There are two practices in this configuration — attacking the institutional and public acceptance of the poor as a disentitled deviant group and organizing to transform the system of opportunities engendering poverty.

Attacking the Institutional and Public Acceptance of the Poor as a Disentitled Deviant Group

Critique of Capitalist Society

There is a strong moral-political critique of a society that is partly blind to its injuries to the disadvantaged, partly self-deceived and misdirected (by its headlong pursuit of its self-interest), and partly knowingly evil and unjust. This critical perspective is the foundation of the action component. Joan is impatient with the proliferating social services, which fragment the client's needs and never helps him or her to understand the root situations that are the mother of need. By contrast she favours "any organization that is helping people to achieve a sense of their own dignity or helping them to do some analysis around their situation. To get a broader overview of their lives in terms of the social structure is helping to do that." The poor would therefore learn to blame the system and not themselves. "The poor are victims," she asserted, "of an economic system that empowers and is sustained by affluent people."

What is the analysis? Donald, a reformist priest-academic and sometimes community activist, gives four causes of poverty. First, the market economy tends to reward those with money and disproportionate access to advantages, such as education, which lead to success. "A market economy tends to emphasize the inequalities that are already present among people." Secondly, the government is not pursuing full employment but has been content to let the unemployment rate rise in order to keep the inflation rate down. "We've got government policy that is willing to pay for reducing inflation or reducing the deficit with the jobs of people. I mean, that's terrible." Thirdly, the tax system in Canada is unfairly biased against the poor. Fourth, public attitudes suggest that if people are poor, it is thought to be their own fault. He imagines the public thinking: "What's the matter with them? Look at what I did with my life; why can't they do that?" Having accepted the faulty assumption that society is inherently fair and gives just rewards for effort, people judge the poor as failures.

The radical analysis is even sharper in its suggestion of concerted action by a corporate-political elite. Joseph puts it plainly: "We think that the politics of poverty is at the same time the politics of wealth, and those who are responsible for building yuppie condominiums and making enormous profits out of an inordinately low minimum wage are the people who are responsible for poverty." Poverty, then, is not simply the haphazard, cumulative result of misconceived, unfair policies. It is the predictable result of a "globalized corporate agenda" that is shaping actions of politicians, bureaucracies and employers in a neo-conservative ideological direction. Corporations as a group are thought to be an almost conspiratorial collective agent shaping the new contours of disadvantage.[138]

---

[138] Corporations which pursue strategies that impact negatively on workers and the poor exist in plenty; I simply think that the notion of a "corporate agenda" actively shaping our lives needs to be "unpacked" and documented and not assumed a priori to have the properties of agents.

Critique of the "Edifice that Confronts the Poor"

If, as a service provider/activist, one is thoroughly convinced of the systemic inequality that produces poverty, then conventional social services take on a contorted, pathological look. After all, minimum wage is a poverty wage, and likewise social assistance benefits simply do not give one enough to live on. Given these reduced circumstances, far from adequate by any community standard, how does one explain the demands placed on the poor by the social services and the charity givers other than the desire to control and stigmatize the poor? As Joseph put it: "All agencies are to one degree or another tainted with the charitable approach, tainted with ... being part of the edifice that confronts the poor, of moralizing and judging and regulating." He compares the present system with the Elizabethan model. People were forced off the land and became vagabonds ("they now call them 'single employables' but they used the term 'vagabonds' in those days," he adds). Wandering around the countryside soon put them into the control of the workhouse, with its enforced discipline. They do not use whips and stocks like they did in that older time, Joseph commented, "but they use the bureaucracy of the welfare department with a viciousness that's really quite close to the Elizabethan model." Another parallel with the time of the Poor Laws — when charity was dispensed in the parish relief system — is the present decentralized patchwork of welfare jurisdictions in municipalities and county councils. Housing, child care and levels of community and case discretion vary with each small unit. Joseph and some of the others would advocate a centralized delivery of social services to enforce common standards with clear and humane rules.

Even reform-oriented consultations with the poor can be experienced as debasing. Low-income friends of Joan that were asked to tell their stories to the Social Assistance Review Commission in the late 1980s became quite cynical. The commissioners were seen as rich people who did not have the interests of the poor in mind. Why should they continue to expose themselves, with their vulnerabilities and their so-called dysfunctions, for yet another audience that wants to find yet another service for them? They may be marginally better off, Joan thought, but they are "worse off in terms of the community they live in, because they've simply been centred out in that community. Their identity has been exposed. They've

been made more vulnerable." It is hard to escape the insight that
Joseph picked up from a minister friend:

> Charity does a lot more for the giver than the receiver — and I
> think that that's absolutely and fundamentally true.

The idea of "opportunity planner" — detached from the benefits
officer and supposedly available to plan employment strategies for
the social assistance client — is greeted with scepticism by the
radical Joseph and caution by the more reformist Joan. Joseph
immediately assumes that, in some way, benefits will be conditional
on participation in the program. He thinks it will act as a "conduit ...
for cheap labour for low wage employers." "Why is there such
pressure from the welfare system on the single employable," he
asks. Because that section of the "social assistance population ...
has the most direct bearing on the questions of wage structure for
the employers." The single employable needs to be prodded,
underpaid and controlled if he is to fill the low wage pockets of
the economy. The assumption here is that the welfare bureau is an
adjunct of the labour market, disciplining and preparing labour for
the worst parts of the secondary sector.

Joan gives a little benefit of the doubt to the work of the
opportunity planner. But it will only work if there are supports in
place to make the low-income person's move into the workforce
feasible:

> But fine, I mean that's a start that deals with one group of people.
> If a mother is able to get herself into the proper housing situation,
> if she's able to access the proper daycare, if she's able to find a
> job that pays a decent wage, if she has a welfare worker who's
> willing to help her coordinate those pieces — then yes, there will
> be some benefit for her.

This deft awareness of the appropriate contextual supports for the
practice of liberty by the social assistance client comes naturally to
a seasoned communitarian/anti-poverty activist like Joan. It is not
as easily grasped or implemented in a bureaucratic system like
Welfare.

The Charity Approach

The approach of the charity-givers evokes moral disgust from
the anti-poverty activists. The charity model says, according to
Joanne, you do not have the right to eat properly at the end of the
month, but rather you must depend on the mercy of the givers.

Accepting this is the first step to a neo-conservative society such as President Reagan envisioned in the 1980s, Donald noted. Let us substitute volunteerism for government programs, Reagan said. Donald thinks that that is the opposite of what we should be working towards. "What should we be working towards?" he was asked. Structures of justice in the economic and political arena, founded on rights, in his view.

The charity approach demeans not only the recipient, but corrupts the affluent. We benefit economically from a group of low-income people who will consume our leftover goods. But most of all it is essential to our feelings of good will on the holidays. The privileged think "that by giving their canned goods away once or twice a year they have really done something to resolve a problem. Whereas it is a perpetuation of the problem which ought not to be necessary" (Joan). The charity model does not change the structure of society. By conferring an emotional and economic function on the poor, it helps maintains people in their poverty.

Critique of the Middle Class

Donald contends that the system that is producing poverty — which is a political, economic and class system — is led by elites, but sustained by the middle class. The middle class, being a privileged group, has a vested interest in the structure of opportunities. It is not surprising, therefore, that this group resists identifying with the poor and making radical reforms. In Joanne's view, "That's a pretty scary thing for a lot of people to look at, particularly when they are working very hard to get the qualifications to maintain the position. It is hard to look at that as a barrier in and of itself." Not wanting to dethrone its advantageous position in the competitive system, and also because it feels that its privileges are under attack, the middle class are not very willing to redistribute rewards and share power with the disadvantaged. Without that willingness, Joan noted:

> I don't think we can simply empower low-income people and say "You change the system." The mainstream must be willing to make changes.

Sometimes people are carried away by emotion when Patricia tells them what is happening, and they pledge action — but it rarely lasts. Her view is that non-poor people do not want to know about the poverty problem. Their reluctance to sustain attention for more than band-aid efforts for change has psychological roots in their desire to evade guilt. If they really knew what was going on, they would have to do something. And if they were not doing anything, they would feel guilty. People do not want guilt gnawing away at their insides — so they move away from the issue. If Patricia's analysis is correct, then the middle class has a vested interest in not only the structure of opportunities but also the structure of ignorance about poverty. Along with managing its presentational requirements in everyday life, middle-class society must also keep its repressions intact.

Organizing to Transform the System of Opportunities Engendering Poverty

The aim here is to act with and on behalf of the poor without being part of the proliferating webs of the poverty industry. Activist/critics in both "D" and "E" configurations are critical of the organizational and professional "business as usual" that is built on the foundation of material deprivation and human suffering. Service provision within the various agencies responds to felt needs of the organization and its abstract reading of situations of poverty. If not involved in making assessments, monitoring, filing and recording poverty, what else would social services personnel do? Service organizations become fiefdoms in the social services field and the pretensions of its workers to professional status are not highly regarded. If you look under many a professional veneer, Joseph noted, you will find the old paternalism towards the poor. He told of a letter in the city newspaper by a social worker whose wallet was stolen during a visit to the Urban Resource Centre, where service providers and low-income people mingle. The letter condemned (according to Joseph) "whichever member of the poor community stole the wallet." Joseph indicated that it could have been a coworker, but the assumption was that here "I'm trying to help these people and here they come along and stab me in the back because they're underserving and they're somehow not appreciative of what I'm doing."

The activists — tending to be loosely tied to organizations — disdain the whole routinization of poverty. The actions engaged in tend to focus on changing the structure in which the poor are enmeshed — taking advantage of new funding possibilities which will create new channels of resource distribution and new rules to organize work and sharing (contrast this with "C," which is helping the poor to play by the current rules). The actions initiated or supported by the activists (in "D" and "E") tend to be new ventures, such as an unemployment drop-in centre, a skills exchange, a worker co-operative of immigrant women producing services, and so on. The more radical, such as Joseph at the London Anti-Poverty Organization, began with one-on-one advocacy in people's individual situations, then expanded to "concentrate pretty well exclusively on more generalized forms of action, mobilizing, lobbying." It is to the actions of this configuration that we now turn.

Dialoguing and Forming Alliances

Dialogic Force Relations

In the Foucauldian perspective, power is studied in ascending order from its local to, potentially, its global formation. At each level, the focus of study is the "force relation" which, especially in liberal society, involves neither total domination nor total submission of the two parties. Instead, the force relation is often a mobile dialogue between unequals. Given that government's task is the governability of the social (a realm of ostensibly free action), its force relations "assumes a 'free subject,' not an individual existing in an essential space of freedom, but one whose subjection is consistent with forms of choice."[139] Part of the great craft of modern bureaucracy is the rhetoric and machinery of consultation and "empowerment." Government power avoids crude domination by "invoking the capacities and powers of the self-governing individual while at the same time undertaking to foster, shape and use those same capacities and powers."[140]

The moderates are far more positive about dialogue and collaboration than the radicals. The vision here is a broad coalition of the poor and those in the middle class and positions of influence in

---

[139] Dean, "'A Social Structure'," 162.

[140] Ibid., 163.

order to improve societal conditions. Joan, for instance, thinks that for a reform movement of poor people to succeed they must be joined by middle income people and a minority, at least, of the powerful. The privileged should be "willing to be in solidarity with low-income people and ... give some leadership of low-income people." There is the hope among the moderates that once an unconstrained dialogue occurs, they can convince the rest of society of the importance of "structures of justice" needed for the peaceful and just society where virtue reigns. In this good society the poor will be empowered by social services, not penalized. They will be able to make their own choices about whether to be educated or to stay home with the children while on benefits. Benefit levels will be brought closer to the poverty line. Their good society, in short, is a reformed, not necessarily non-capitalist, society.

Radical Positions

There may be a need for social workers and social programs to continue to exist in the radical idea of the good society, because short-term sufferings need to be alleviated. But the basic development of the individual and the eradication of the problems of disadvantage requires a massive mobilization of people to win economic, political and social opportunities for the poor. Low-income people need to join with their allies in the labour unions and popular movements so that they can (in Joseph's words) "actually go out and confront the powers that be to try to win concessions, to try to win changes necessary, to try to hold the line on cutback measures, etc." The radical vision is of a socialist society "in which those who produce all the wealth in this society at the same time own and control it" (Joseph). He exhorts the poor to recall the radical traditions of the unemployed protestors of the Thirties and to rise up with their allies and confront the imposing edifice of power. Knowing that poverty erodes people's energy and hope to mobilize and protest, Joseph wants to be part of the catalyst that will help them rise up.

Low-income people in the anti-poverty movement must make alliances. They need to ally with the social movements, such as the women's and environmental movements, as well as the churches and supportive social agencies. It is by sharing facilities, resources, and skills with such people and organizations in the community that anti-poverty groups have stayed alive.[141] Beyond the community, such alliances form the basis of regional and national coalitions of unions and community groups that showed their organizing mettle at the March on Poverty of 1989 (to Queens Park, Toronto) and at the large political demonstrations against the Conservative government in Ottawa in the late 1980s and the Peterson government in Ontario.[142] Among the organizations that supported and helped to organize these demonstrations were: Greenpeace, Ontario Federation of Students, Toronto Disarmament Network, Native organizations, National Action Committee on the Status of Women, Ontario Secondary School Teachers Federation, Ontario Farmers Union, Building Trades Council, Public Service Alliance of Canada, Canadian Union of Postal Workers, disabled groups and many more.

One of the most important alliances to be made is with the trade union movement. After all, poor people's organizations lack the lever of withdrawing their labour that unionists have. On its own, community organizing cannot defeat the corporate attack on people's livelihoods. It must join forces with the unions that protect the interests of working men and women in thousands of workplaces.

They must not engage in phony dialogues with the rich and established, whose exploitation of the poor put them beyond the pale of useful co-operation. Joseph grasps the co-opting nature of dialogue and rejects it: "We've always been unashamedly in favour of confronting the people responsible for the suffering of the poor rather than seeking to sit on committees with them and pretend that we're all on the same side and we all have a common set of interests. We don't think we do."

How can one dialogue with someone who pretends to be concerned with your well-being but treats his daily exploitation of you as a given that is beyond discussion? Pretending to share interests with the privileged, when their very defence of their privileges is keeping you poor, is dishonest; it is more honest to engage in struggle. Joseph wants to disentangle his followers from

---

[141] Clarke, "Ontario's social movements," 217.

[142] Ibid., 218-221.

the disempowering webs of dialogue set up by the powerful. "We do have to actually instill in people a certain combativity. And so, no, I don't think we can work within. I don't think we all can work together. I think most can work against poverty, but there are some who are not going to."

Confronting the Powers that Be

The problem is no longer the poor, but it is how we combat irresponsible moneyed elites and their political representatives. The politics of poverty, for the critics and activists of configuration "E," is at the same time the politics of wealth. The foes are the elites that build the condominiums which displace the housing of the poor, the employers who build fortunes out of their workers' minimum wages, and the politicians who serve the interests of the rich. What are some of the confrontations between poor people and the elites? Anti-poverty groups in the mid-1980s mobilized around the demand for a 25 percent increase in sub-poverty social assistance benefits and brought it forward to the Ontario government. The government refused it. This had a galvanizing effect in extending the protesting network throughout the province. Mothers and Others Making Change in Kitchener demanded standards of fairness from their local food bank. Other groups organized to demand a clothing allowance for children on welfare.[143]

Joseph was involved in the organizing of single mothers who were threatened by the loss of hydro in their homes. These mothers went down to the Public Utilities Commission and confronted the officials of the utility to demand that these repressive actions against the poor cease. Joseph's account suggests that anti-poverty politics tries to convert despair to anger, which is projected outward from the self towards the confronted enemy.

> We are able to organize an action where single mothers go down to the public utilities commission. And these fat bastards who never have been challenged in their lives by such upstarts are actually confronted by eloquent, passionate, angry statements from people who've never before spoken out in any kind of public forum. I mean that filled me with an enthusiasm that is just unstoppable.

---

[143] Ibid., 217.

We start to see what Joseph is getting out of organizing the poor. He is seeing the exercise of virtue and courage standing up against both the poor's, and *his*, enemies in authority.

> People don't have to suffer in silence. People can fight back and it's the most important thing to do in a system that seems to me to be based on oppressing people; fighting back is not just a duty, it's an enormous happiness.

He recalled hearing a talk from an organizer of the unemployed back in the Great Depression, who said there is nothing shameful in being poor or jobless because it is the system and the politicians that are responsible for that. But if you are prepared to watch your children go hungry, and not do anything about it, that is when you should be ashamed. Joseph found that to be profoundly true. The only way to have dignity when you're robbed of everything, he noted, "is to say that 'No, I'm just not prepared to tolerate it, and it's not just my problem. It's a problem of all my brothers and sisters and we are going to fight for something better.'"

This man is romanticizing the poor and wants to organize a movement which will embody the virtues that he finds essential to his moral and political being. But these motives become a catalyst for the organization. Joseph's fusion of his moral vision and his organizing feeds into a powerful need of the low-income people who accept his leadership. In sacrificing for a wider cause than their own troubles, poor members gain personal and group *self-respect* (and self-efficacy). A class with self-respect is more likely to want to engage in politics than one without. Joseph's language and conviction about courage, faith, and solidarity — and the confrontations to which he applies them — are building collective self-respect among the poor, which fuels a sense of entitlement that brings them to larger goals. As Miller writes, "collective self-respect, then, is a political act in gaining it and a political action in using it."[144] Providers' visions (like Colleen's, in the previous chapter), however romantic, can release a powerful conditioning current which helps the recipients to, proactively, break the self-isolating shell of poverty.

---

[144] Miller, "Poverty and respect," 29.

Difficulties of Organizing the Poor

While such forms of collective and political action are an important component in fighting injustices, for many living in poverty such direct and open acts of confrontation are too frightening and inappropriate. Low-income people who have internalized society's message that blames the poor for their poverty will simply lack the sense of self-efficacy to join. Many poor struggle with stigma and shame, and their desire for anonymity does not welcome the public protests and story-telling of an anti-poverty movement.

Without access to conventional sources of power, poverty militants often take up "disruptive" techniques of protest. The established powers respond with their powerful weapon of ascribing unrespectability. They convince the public that people who would indulge in such upsetting tactics are not very respectable or worthy of serious consideration. This places a stigma on the protestors and on those who would want to join them. The mainstream — with its access to government and media — has other methods of neutralizing the poor. From the perch of respectability and impartiality which establishment groups and figures are granted by the media, they label anti-poverty groups as just another squabbling "special interest" which, being out of the mainstream, needs to be treated with caution.

Conclusion

The value of the "E" perspective is to complete the journey begun by the communitarians; i.e., to take the problem of poverty out of the little black box of social services and into the economic domain which is its generator. It is in the economy that the conflict between personal rights (which include welfare and civil rights) and property rights is waged.[145] It is in the economy that the casualty of that conflict we know as "poverty" is produced. The state's role in liberal-capitalist regimes is ambiguous. Though the Canadian state flirted with the idea of full employment and a commitment to a guaranteed adequate income for all citizens, it backed off. Today it

---

[145] Bowles and Gintis, *Democracy*, 102.

plays an ancillary role to the market, providing a (fraying) safety net for those who are vulnerable. While the state still provides a foundation for citizens' rights, its means of monitoring how they play out in the economy are ineffective and underfunded. The radicals refuse to limit the horizon of the disadvantaged's project to the social services network. Investing your hopes for the eradication of poverty in the latter is like expecting to win a war by taking over the medical corps which administers to the wounded. To struggle effectively for personal rights, we must be in the proper battlefield, the radicals say. The economy should be converted from the private to the public sphere. "This means," according to Bowles and Gintis, "democratic economic planning, public controls, regulation of the use and disposition of private productive property and, under some conditions, nationalization."[146] In more immediate terms, it means defending the wages, benefits and job security of men and women in the labour force against the downsizing efforts of the elites. The value of the contribution of working men and women is being systematically degraded by the breaking up of full-time work and the payment of low wages for the new service jobs. In short, the real problem is how to end the production of poverty in the formative domain of market incomes; it is *not* how to end pauperism as a part of a project of socialization of the "discontinuous" elements in the dominant order.

The activists and critics in "E" know that they must interact with people in the social services, but they do not want to identify with their self-serving project. After all, by the state's refusal to back full employment and its self-limitation of its redistributive role and by the system's failure to provide enough in social wages to provide a decent living, it is ensuring that people will continue to rely on the cadre of service providers in the social services system. It is priming the pump of the poverty industry. More and more services are found out to be needed, more and more workers gain their identities from the provision of services, and more and more people get burned out by the need of yet more services, staff and funding. The sheer individualism of the social services approach guarantees

---

[146] Ibid.

its inefficient, wrong-headed response to the structural-economic nature of poverty.

Finally, there is an impatience with the psychologism of the earlier role configurations, as though the poor were puzzles to be finally (and gratifyingly) solved with the magic tool of empathy. The anti-poverty and communitarian people look at what is happening in a militantly sociopolitical way. There is an economic crisis that is propagating disadvantage like a plague. Let us give people what they need, non-judgmentally, and have them join us in the real struggle of providing the wherewithal for a decent living for all.

Criticisms of "E"

Once again, a romantic view of the poor emerges, conceiving their class anger to be a sword that can cut through the corruption of inequality. Predictably, the idealizations lead to real blindnesses. For example, Joseph apparently does not see retraining and education as key aspects of the poor's empowerment. He mistrusts these goals when they are enunciated by conventional society because they are tainted by their association with the "blaming the victim" perspective which he despises. "We don't consider poverty or unemployment to be something that flows from personal inadequacy or a lack of education or training *per se.*" As stated, we know what he means, but does he think the poor do not need skill-building, literacy instruction, job retraining and education? Is he prevented by his militant view from seeing that some of the problems of poor people in labour markets are due to mismatches between their skills and the demands of the jobs on offer (not all of which are low-paying)? The radical risks delegitimizing the small empowerments that are available to low-income people from the training system. As well, by refusing to respect that system, he has forfeited his right to influence it.

Perhaps the reason the radical delegitimizes training and redistributive programs that offer small gains to low-income people is that they may make the poor satisfied (or at least passively accepting). The ambitious agenda of social change which the radical wants may be better served if the contradictions in the distributive system stand out so glaringly that the poor are stirred to fight the obvious indignities imposed on them. But the *a priori* negation operating here may deprive the anti-poverty poor of small gains which will alleviate their sufferings. It is doubtful that they should be ideologically prevented from using the system for their own (admittedly individualistic) benefit.

The anti-poverty route has high costs and risks associated with it, for organizer and member. The risks to members is that they might get arrested or feel the stigma of being publicly associated with a radical group; later, there could be repercussions in the search for work and respectability. As well, collective action is exhausting, stressful and uncertain of success.

The leader calls fellow combatants to a struggle for human dignity, where what is gained accrues to collective strength and solidarity. But class society hands out its rewards to *individuals* ultimately — and what will keep the members committed after they gain their own individual success?

Having presented the role configurations of service providers, we now turn to the responses and orientations to the social services and action field by low-income informants themselves.

8

Receiving and Acting

*I*n Chapter 2, we looked at the stresses and contingencies bearing down on poor people outside of the Social Services and Actions (SSA) field; i.e., in market and community relations. The task in this final chapter is to explore low-income informants' reactions to the whole system of helping and activating which they come in contact with in their hours of need (and that we have presented in the last five chapters). Drawing from the sampling of low-income informants in this study, comments (in order of prominence) tended to focus on state bureaucracies, food-providing institutions, charity organizations and anti-poverty groups.

The chapter, broadly speaking, has two parts. The first ("receiving") has to do with the expressed reactions to being recipients in the SSA field. The final part ("acting") presents an account of the practices in which informants engage to reproduce, to protect themselves from, and to transform the social relations of poverty.

An orienting question of the first part is: What are the meanings people in need ascribe to the services that they see as important to their well-being? To those who might ask *why* low-income people's meanings are important in the first place, there are even some system-conforming reasons why this is so. Social administrators assume that the benefits of being a service recipient outweigh the costs. But for many services, the assumption is wrong — and you can only learn this from free-flowing discourse with recipients who will recount, chapter and verse, the high costs to self and social reputation of the various services. But, even more than that, client perceptions and evaluations of social service programs are extremely valuable input against which official records and assessments can be checked. Checking caseworker notes against client notes reduces error, shows the worker and official where organizational problems may be generating dysfunction, and gives a better chance to the recipient to ensure that their rights are being continually articulated for the helping agency.

There is, of course, a more radical reason for recipient input. If the premise for help is shifted from client deficit to the exclusionary patterns of economy and community, then recipient input is a necessary dialogue for ensuring that people get what they need. Need-articulation is now more a political matter, and hearing the needs of economic victims (as opposed to just professionally assessing them) is an essential act of inclusion that is prologue to the more profound integration of the poor into the resources and powers of the majority. We have to consider the possibility that affluence makes us relatively ignorant of how social structure conditions the freedom of the market winner and the unfreedom of the market loser. The voices of the poor, fully heard through legitimate, participatory channels, may make it less essential for them to rely on the empathy of the providers.

In this "receiving" part of the chapter, there are three parts: "living an administered life," "coping with stigma and disrespect," and "receiving food from others."

Living an Administered Life

Being "On the System"

There were certainly a small number of informants who praised their caseworkers. But the more prevalent impression was that workers in the public system seemed not to grasp the contextual factors bearing on the poor. Brenda, a single mother, found that her social worker acted mechanically, looking to a book for answers rather than relating to her as a human being. "I think it should be mandatory," she commented, "for everyone who wants to work in social services to live in poverty for a year. How can they help when they don't know what it is like?"

While on government benefits, Stephanie noted, one was a dependent of "the system." The informants know that the system is far less responsive to client demand than the marketplace is for the person with money. One is contending with organizational prioritizing, scarce manpower, and just the generally slower time frame of bureaucratic operations. This powerful, intractable, many-headed phenomenon supplied not only goods and services that one could not afford on the market, but worked like a magnetic field into which one was drawn against one's will. For instance, getting a loan on the private market is difficult for someone on Mother's Allowance. Being discriminated against at the bank throws people back, by default, onto public subsidy. A case in point is George on Disability. At one point, he needed money for gas to get from his home in St. Thomas to Fanshawe College for his courses. "This money had to be borrowed. [From the government?] Naturally. Eventually I have to pay it back."

Being "on the system" means waiting in line for administered services. Stephanie thought that being perpetually stuck on a waiting list in some sense defined the condition of the low-income person. For every single resource she and her family needed during the time of a family break-up in Ottawa — from legal help, to physical examination for sexual molestation, to psychiatric and emotional help, to housing — they were on a waiting list. In London, she found, at least they talk to you while you are on the list, but not in Ottawa. In another instance, young single mother Michele waited to get into subsidized housing; now that she is in, she has waited three years for new windows and for her unit to be painted.

Being Scrutinized and Appraised

Low-income informants find that service providers invade their privacy. Near the end of the month, Michele sometimes has to go to the Food Bank if she can find transportation. She will *not* go to a particular religious charity and women's hostel, however, because "it is too degrading." They question her about why she cannot afford to buy food, what she does with her money, and why she was there. "And you're going, 'Hey, look at my bills'." By contrast, other groups and organizations just update your files, neither asking questions nor condemning. "They never condemn what you're doing to survive and, at times, it is really rough to survive."

The predominant attitude towards invasion of privacy was negative. Dan found that although the government seems to want to know everything about you, they do not know anything about how you live. "The government think they know everything, but they don't know enough. They don't know how we live, don't know where, … or what we live on, what we do." Sandra points scornfully at the ignorance of young, childless government officials from

Children's Aid advising her on childbirth. It is not that the govern-ment is ignorant, of course; it is, rather, that the knowledge they seek is knowledge for control and assessment purposes, rather than humane assistance. It is power knowledge, drawn for different reasons and uses than the communicative discourse coming out of the lifeworld.

Another response to state invasion of privacy is to internalize its gaze into one's own self-monitoring. Some people felt the state's presence as an embodiment of the Generalized Other; in effect, a moral deputy of the wider society. George received a travel subsidy that allowed him to pursue his courses at a community college. He felt morally obligated to use the money responsibly, interpreted it as a sacred trust (as from a parent). Possibly he is just being honourable, but he and others felt the watchful public eye even when they were alone with their families. Many single parents do not feel personally entitled to spend much of their benefits on themselves. They regarded their family benefits as given to them because they have children, so they feel that they cannot easily spend public money on their own nutrition (as though government was internalized as a kind of Big Brother).

Informants are wary of continuing to tell their story to all kinds of providers and questioners. When Sandra got a flier from Joseph's anti-poverty organization, she ran into friends who had been there. They told her, "'Don't go. It's not worth it. They make you get up and degrade yourself." The organization, it was felt, made people "talk about their personal life." Even if the purpose was political and progressive, the humiliation effect might end up being the same. And, of course, not just providers but social researchers want the story of the poor. We also have an instrumentalist intent, though we want to give expression to her personal agency as well. Beth told the interviewer from our study after it was over: "I guess your interest in me must be for the study." Not being sure of any gain (in this case she wanted friendship), Beth was expressing the chagrin of a class which was always the one being written about in other people's narratives, but never the writer.

In the face of this invasion of personal knowledge, it is vital to exercise whatever control you have over who finds out about your poverty. If possible, you want to keep the knowledge out of the hands of your community. Michele spoke about not wanting to get food baskets from her affluent church: "They don't know you're there until you tell them and I refuse to tell them." This underscores the importance of anonymity in the provision of emergency relief, without which many eligible persons will not show up for the help they need.

Being Controlled; Feeling Powerless

The instances of being and feeling powerless are abundant in the interviews. One area of particular difficulty was housing. Albert was on welfare when his worker found out that, when he was employed full-time, he had begun negotiating to buy a house from his boss at specially reduced mortgage rates. The worker cut him off benefits instantly saying that he could not buy a house and expect welfare.

Where does one live? For some there is a forced choice situation of living in either subsidized housing or in the private sector without enough food to eat. Seventy-year old Julia, pressured by financial difficulty into public housing for seniors, feels "caged and helpless." Now that the subsidized housing laws have changed to integrate over-65s with ex-psychiatric patients, she and the older people in her building are too afraid to use the common areas any more — for fear of mingling with the former patients. Other informants as well, living without the controls and familiarity of cohesive neighbourhoods, felt powerless in their housing situations. People complained of the absence of smoke alarms in their complex, the vandalism, the false fire alarms, the stabbing incidents, the thefts and burglaries, the dirt, and the cockroaches and other insects. People feel bunkered in their units, fearful of drug abusers, drug dealers and teen gangs.

Some feel trapped in their marginal jobs. For instance, Kevin cannot quit his low-paying and unsafe job at the mall's photography store because he would face at least a 6-week wait for UI (and retraining). (That was before the UI rules tightened to exclude all voluntary quits.) His company refuses to lay him off. Caught between a rock and a hard place, Kevin is stuck without meaningful options. He cannot abide Welfare: "I'm a very proud person. I couldn't sit back … and just go on Welfare. I couldn't do that. I have to work; I have to provide for myself. I have to take care of myself. I couldn't let somebody else take care of me. It would drive me crazy. It would drive me absolutely up the wall."

This feeling and reality of being powerless is at the heart of being poor. Sandra spoke of it plainly and without illusion.

> What can you do? Who are you going to go to to get out of this? You go to somebody, you talk to them. "Well, we'll see what we can do about it." How long does it take? Your lifetime? You end up dying where you are because you can't get the help you need.

The external control never lets up for the long-term poor, only shifts its locus from time to time. As market freedoms and deregulation increase, the people defeated by the market become, in Panitch's words, "regulated and policed and judged as welfare agencies and courts — those quintessential state apparatuses — do not empty but rather fill up."[147]

Being Constrained by Disincentives

Bureaucratic subsidies are riddled with disincentives to find a market job and income that will get you off the system. George's wife has decided not to work as long as George is in school, because her earnings (in excess of $150 a month, in 1989) will be taken off her husband's cheque. When George did extra work to "keep his hand in" in the mental health field, even earning below the allowable $150 dollars a month, it later resulted in a major reduction of a grant for his education. Suitably "chastened," George stopped working. In another case, Louise's disability pension does not allow her to work without losing dollars from her small benefit cheque. She yearns to be with other people in the workplace. Similarly, Albert with his two children chafes at the $150 limit of allowable "free" earnings, for he wishes to make more money in the workplace. The subsidized poor are hemmed in with restrictions.

Enablements carried a double edge for the recipients of Family Benefits. One is entitled to a dental card, a drug card, a clothing allowance, prescription glasses and many other supports. If the person decides to work full-time at a low-wage job, benefits will be cut and expenses increased. Given the fact that most new jobs in recent years are low-paying and part-time, and that child care is

---

[147] Panich, "Changing Gears," 39.

often not available, there is no incentive to find work. To an active, ambitious woman in this situation such as Nancy, one either festers in such a system or one seeks education, as she is doing.

> It's crazy, like I mean right now the incentive to go out and work for me is like practically zippo. Because if I work they're going to put my rent up ... and I will have a lot less money at the end ... It's not making it even semi-attractive to go out and get a job. I mean, why do you think I'm here studying? So I can get a better paying job and then move out altogether if possible.

Benefits for such a woman make sense in the context of a life plan, not as the furnishing of a state-supported enclave.

There are further ambiguities in state support, as when one can be made to feel entitled by one branch of the bureaucracy but disentitled by another — trusted and mistrusted. This is George's story. When transportation assistance from his town to a community college was provided by the government, George took it as evidence that they believed in him. Bus money had taken food from his family's table, so the aid here was particularly cherished. "The motivation was within, but it gave me the push I needed — in the right direction." He added revealingly: "If they were willing to trust me that much, I was willing to put in the effort." Trust here is a part of George's implicit exchange, or contract, with the government.

Yet, when it was discovered that he had done some part-time work in the previous year (something he had already reported to a worker and forgotten), he was yanked dramatically out of line at the community college. His grant money was quickly reduced by the amount he had earned. The discovery of the disqualifying part-time work was seized upon with suspicious sharpness, as though it were the looked-for result of a routinely mistrustful scrutiny. Overall, George has received mixed messages from a disjointed bureaucratic system, something which will undoubtedly temper his own idealistic reactions towards the state.

Coping with Stigma and Disrespect

Respect is a social resource. When we are disrespected, we lose the right to expect civility from others who are free to exploit and dominate us without guilt or social sanction. As Miller indicates, "those deemed 'different' or 'less worthy,' whether it is because they are believed to be incompetent, improvident, workshy ... are regarded as undeserving and available for social and economic denigration."[148] The public holds disrespectful stereotypes about the poor which are simply untrue. It is thought in some circles that poor people are not badly off because most of them are students, or they benefit from subsidized child care or shelter allowances. The facts say different: just 5 percent of all low-income people are students, 5 percent receive child care subsidies, and 19 percent get some form of rental subsidy. It is thought that having a job brings families out of poverty. But one-third of working-age poor families have had a full year of employment. It is thought that poverty is only a temporary state that people move in and out of. But more than 40 percent of poor people in a given year will remain poor for at least five years. It is thought that being poor is a result of being unskilled and illiterate. But there is a rapid increase in the rate of poverty among well-educated families: 29 percent of poor families have members with some post-secondary education, more than double the percentage of ten years ago. It is thought that the poor are sycophants, living off their income tax. But many of the poor work or want to work and take pride in paying taxes. In Albert's words, "I am a citizen, I pay taxes — I am not a welfare bum."

Coming back to the lived experience of our informants, many of them, especially the single mothers, feel disrespect in their everyday encounters. Even though Kate, a single mother, had gone back to school, she still felt less of a person because she received government assistance. When she and her sister went apartment-hunting and drove by a subsidized housing complex, her sister commented: "Even *you* deserve better than this." Perhaps it was the sister's unspoken assumption that stung here: "being second-class, you should not expect to live in a pleasant environment like average people."

The incivility was even more marked in Judith's case. Ever since she has gone on Mother's Allowance during the last year she has felt a definite change in how people treat her. She lives is a normal rental unit with her two children, paying about 80% of her income on rent. When her rent went up by $21.00 and she could not afford

---

[148] Miller, "Poverty and respect," 17-18.

to pay it, her worker gave her approximately 23 cents which brought her to her maximum limit. The loss of that $21.00 meant no entertainment or recreation money. Her worker's response is always: "We're terribly sorry. You'll have to make do." Judith finds it odd that her worker is paid to tell her, "Can you leave me alone?" In another instance of disrespect, when she was at the bank once and did not balance things correctly, the female bank teller called her "stupid." She cannot get a credit card or get a lease because she is on Mother's Allowance — all of which conveys to her that she is a second-class citizen. In Judith's bitter summation: "when you're a housewife, you're garbage. We're lower than the native Canadian people."

While on social benefits, it feels as if the whole of society mistrusts you. Possessing a discreditable stigma, one always runs the risk of finding either a real or a projected moral disapproval from others. Having a mistrustful generalized "other" looking over one's shoulder means that, even interiorly, one must appease, win over, or defy a presumption of unworthiness. Unlike the non-deviant employed person, who is presumed worthy, the social assistance recipient is presumed unworthy until proven worthy. Hiding the empirical marks of one's deviant status is a daily concern.

It is in this context that we can understand the informants' dislike of public housing. Passing as normal is immensely more difficult if you are segregated in your housing or at school. People felt marked by their address. "Don't tell them your address," Julia urged. "You say _____ Street, and they know you live in subsidized housing." Brenda lived in a subsidized area in north London for a few months and was too embarrassed to get off at her bus stop. She finally left subsidized housing but is now unable to eat very well because of the higher rent she has to pay for her private apartment. Why did she flee public housing, which would seem to go against her rational self-interest? Because public housing is a zone of disrespect that would taint both her and her two boys. Segregating the poor in housing or in daily life not only shows disrespect but, in fact, promotes disrespect. The social distance thus created is a breeding ground of societal stereotypes, rumours and anxieties. When in segregated areas, the poor are isolated from information and useful employment contacts, making unemployment more probable. The joblessness in turn feeds into the public stereotype that the poor are "shiftless" and unwilling to work. One is caught up in a self-reinforcing loop (or trap) of disrespect and disadvantage. Given the saliency of the poor in segregated areas or situations, it is not surprising that Stephanie, for instance, castigates welfare recipients who abuse alcohol or drugs or do not buy enough food for their children. Their undisciplined consumption makes her look bad: "I'm not a drinker ... When I see things like that, it makes me more angry, because people classify me as that. And there's no way, I want to be out there working."

Receiving Food from Others

To meet the needs of this hungry constituency, various non-market food outlets and programs have arisen, including food banks, soup kitchens and food baskets from churches and other organizations. Using these public system outlets introduces a new strategic requirement for the recipients, different in kind from those on the marketplace. What is the cost to one's self-respect that is exacted by the various outlets? What indignities must a person avoid to retain pride and belief in his- or herself as well as keep a good standing with his or her children? We now look at the respondents' perceptions about what was positive or negative about these food outlets.

Food Banks

The increase in food outlets has brought more opportunity for the marginal poor person to slip out of the control nexus and exercise some choice. So Robert, an older single man, goes to the food bank each month and eats at the soup kitchen four or five times a week. Every three months, he receives a food basket from a religious benefit society. Having learned to live with his marginality, he has considerable choice of food venues, eats well, and is rather content. With the larger number of outlets, people have more choice. They can avoid the more controlling food services — with their somewhat intrusive screening, and religious and counselling requirements — and can try to minimize the costs to the self. This "working the system," while odious to organizations that want to manage the poor, may be one way of preserving dignity, making choices that are flexibly attuned to hard times, and reducing dependency. (From this standpoint the computerization of outlets and low-income users may be seen to decrease options and increase social control over low-income persons.)

But unambivalent appreciation for the outlets was rare. Many, but not all, who found the food banks tolerable had children (though some mothers refused to go). An enabling factor in their going was their sense of parental responsibility. Single father Albert was firm in asserting that food banks are a necessity when you do not have enough to feed your children. "Pride has no place in that situation." Therefore he has "no qualms about going ... 'God helps those that help themselves'." He criticized others who are too proud to make use of the outlets.

> You've got St. Paul Cathedral, they give out food, the Salvation Army, the Food Bank, St. Vincent de Paul. With all these places for food for free, it's just there for the asking. There's no need to go hungry. Anybody that cries the blues because they have no food in the house and won't go to those places, I have no pity on them.

George, a father in his thirties, agreed: when there is nothing in the house and you have children, you must seek food. "It's not a matter of begging, it's a matter of: 'Look, you know, there's a definite need here'."

But overall there was a negative reaction to food banks. People would hold back as a matter of pride (e.g., Brenda). The idea of food banks, to others such as Mark, was demeaning and incredible ("I can't believe that it's happening"). Dan has been to food banks and feels himself degraded by the experience:

> I feel myself a cheap old bugger because, I figure, the help that I have I should be able to work [for] — and I shouldn't be able to cry on food banks or any around here that's got food.

The need to feed the children demands a sacrifice of pride and self-respect. "Foolish pride can sometimes get in your way," George said, "that says, 'Look, you know, I'm too good for that.' ... Pride kind of goes back here [gesturing behind him, chuckling ruefully]. If it means that you have to ask, you have to ask." The sense of degradation is perhaps partly lessened by the pride taken in one's parenting but is hardly comparable to the optimal situation of independently providing for one's children.

People felt demeaned when they were processed in a public, visible way by an organization. Stephanie found that the place where she had to wait for an organization's food basket totally set her apart, in a kind of showcase. She wanted to wait near the offices, where she might be taken for a normal person, even a worker. She sat exposed, feeling that people knew why she was there, imagining them thinking: "Ha, she's going in there, she's no good." The physical environment of the agency had put her into a situation which she described as "very embarrassing, very low, very degrading." Stephanie expressed the cost to the recipient not in money but in social status and self-respect. This is not something abstract but is felt in the body, in the reactions of stress, in the burning shame of being needful within the critical gaze of the public.

Another respondent was waiting in a queue for Christmas food and found that she was being filmed as a part of the organization's public relations endeavour.

Soup Kitchens, Churches

People avoided crossing a line that might irreparably degrade their self-understanding and status. The threshhold of the soup kitchen was one such line. In fairness, the soup kitchen was praised by an activist as a social gathering place and a community builder, and a few respondents approved of it. But being there seemed to enact an underclass role drawn from people's images of the Depression. Many respondents thought of it as beneath their dignity. In tones of fervent relief, they said they had managed to stay out of the soup kitchen. "Hopefully," said Peter, "I'll never have to go to the soup kitchen ... I guess everyone has some degree of pride and it's beyond me at the moment. I can't see myself going there. I walked there one time with a friend, but I just couldn't. I just left." Nancy commented in a similar spirit: "I've never eaten in a soup kitchen. I've been extremely lucky that way."

When the informants were asked about receiving help from churches, the response was negative. The anonymous, even impersonal, receiving of food from an organization to which you are a stranger was thought to be better than getting help from your church. One's own church should not be putting food on one's table. After all, the church is in part a status community, and the begging produces a sharp reduction in status. "It's a question of pride," Michele said. "They don't know you're there unless you tell them and I refuse to tell them. And yet I belong to a very affluent church. But I refuse."

George, on the other hand, *has* gone to his church for food a few times and it was not pleasant. The church scrutinized him closely, in comparison with the food bank which was positively circumspect. "It is degrading," he found, "it is very degrading for a person to have to ask in the first place — but then to be put to the third degree ... The church is the last place that I would go to ask for food." One slides down from the status of a regular church member to that of a charity case. George does not want to present himself to others in a way that brings shame and disrespect to him and his family. "You like to have an image that holds up ... It's different on spiritual matters ... It shouldn't be like that, maybe it's me." Yes, it *is* him he is talking about; it is his self.

The more general point is that service providers for the hungry may need to project a non-intrusive impersonality which respects recipients' privacy and their already mortified identities. Tactful help requires minimizing the needs of the provider's ego and the organization's self-promotion so that food may be given that nourishes the low-income person and not diminishes him.

Informants' Practices

To recapitulate, the situation of the informants and other low-income persons in the society is structured by at least three processes. First, there are the material constraints bearing down on the poor — chiefly unemployment, underemployment, the growth of low-wage jobs, inadequate government benefits, the need for transportation in the city and the lack of low-cost housing. Second, there is the structuring imposed by the administered life where service providers, especially state officials, intrude on private facts, monitor behaviour, decide what you will earn and who will be your neighbours. Thirdly, there is the stigmatized life where people will make social judgments about you based on where you live and will feel they can monitor your spending and behaviour. The question taken up now is, given this environment of social structuring, which positions and practices of the respondents tend to reproduce their subordinate situation, and which express personal agency and even point to transformation of the situation of poverty? We deal first with reproductive practices.

Reproductive Practices

Playing the Game

One reproductive practice is playing the game or "giving them what they want." This cynical, though understandable, strategy was well expressed by a disabled student, Mark.

> I know that having gone through social services that there is a way [to be considered] a more desirable rehabilitative client [and] then you're more likely to get the services faster. Play the game ... You can be labelled pretty fast as a deviant sort of person for society, so learn how to tell the people that you're talking to what they want to know, to make you look better ...

This is not a happy strategy for him, for later he endorsed a model of help based on need, and criticized the service providers who expected the proper presentation of self.

People feel browbeaten into taking a politically neutered stance, which often expresses itself in silence. They talk of sitting back quietly, not complaining. The low self-efficacy of the poor both produces and is produced by silence and passivity. Brenda acts in such a passive way as to virtually disengage her autonomous personal agency. "I'm not used to standing up for myself. I'm used to saying 'I'm on Mother's Allowance' and sitting back quietly." This silence is the acceptance of disentitlement from citizenship and normal discourse. "I'm not involved in politics," she went on. "I isolate myself. There are resources but I don't use them." From this passivity issues defeatism. Speaking of a desire to move to improve his material life with Sandra, Dan said: "I'll probably be denied that too. I've been denied everything else." They have never known anything else but poverty.

Project Feelings about Being Dependent onto Others

People were, as low-income citizens, disentitled — but they projected their felt disentitlement onto others more widely than was justified. Here is Stephanie's reading of the people around her:

> It's almost as if you get the feeling — and *it may only be one-sided* — you get the feeling that people think you're robbing off the system. If you were at least out there working, they look

at you differently. I find people looked at me differently, and I
felt so differently ... going to university, trying to go to university,
people looked at me differently, even at the medical centre.
(emphasis added)

She went on to imagine taxpayer's views:

If we were taxpayers we would probably be heard more than we
are, because a lot of people who are paying their taxes say, "Hey,
we're paying for you to live. Quit complaining."

Even conceding its grounding in reality, she seems aware that she
is projecting. But the angle of vision from her stigmatized enclave
("single mother on benefits") turned particular others into projective
screens on which are read what seems like the judgments of the
whole culture. The problem is less that one cannot interpret others
as just themselves, as it is allowing the assumption of a socially
rejecting public to emasculate your political, social and personal
identity. "We're paying for you, therefore you must not criticize,
protest, even act as a citizen." The projection on the taxpayer is
disempowering, as though what we low-income people have is by
sufferance of the real citizens. See also how she links a presumptive
social identity with her own personal identity: "people looked at
me differently, and I felt so differently ... " Poverty may make one
so hungry for social legitimation that the social judge is thought to
reside within all others; one's low-income self, even when more of
a victim by than an author of its misfortune, cannot sense its own
legitimacy.

Invidious Comparison; Racism

The final reproductive element shown in the interviews was the
attitude of racial prejudice. Daniel and Sandra are superintendents
of a housing complex of low-income people, many of whom are
recently-arrived Cambodian refugees. In return for their accommodation in the complex and a small wage, they are responsible for
keeping the place clean and orderly. This mandate places them in
an uncomfortable and somewhat servile contact with people and
families of alien language and customs, who are going through
traumatic family dislocations, grief and culture shock. Not being
able to choose their neighbours, they must not only live with this
turbulent diversity but clean up its mess. In private, they project
their class anger and sense of powerlessness in prolonged invidious
comparisons with the "pampered" new arrivals, who have entitle-

ments that they themselves do not have. A small sampling of their racist talk:

SANDRA: It's disgusting, it's *sick*, the way some people have to live when they shouldn't really have to live that way.

DANIEL: And another thing is, my father is very … pissed off about this because number one: my dad shot down these guys in the war, the Vietnamese. My dad is a very prejudiced guy against these people. He shot them down and what the hell's happening now? They're bringing them back into Canada.

SANDRA: They have basically taken over … where he was born and raised. They've basically taken over … and that's where his parents live. And then there's the Cami plants in Ingersol, the Japs have basically taken it over.

Prejudice of this sort is ugly, ignorant, and paranoid — and reduces the solidarity of low-income people. But this alienated discourse needs to be decoded. It is symptomatic of an underlying frustration at being handed reduced options — in this case, having to do the dirty work on the fractious front line of interracial contact. As in many other instances in our welfare state — which seems consensualist but is actually divisive — piecemeal policies favouring one group generate disadvantages and competitive strains for another.

Proactive Practices of Personal and Collective Agency

Informants also engaged in proactive practices which sustained their self-identities and projected present activity into a future beyond poverty. I have grouped them under the headings of personal agency and self-empowerment; desire to work; education; making their own narrative; building social connections, and "owning" social benefits. Following that, I look at resistant practices, both individual and collective.

Personal Agency; Self-Empowerment

The resistance to poverty often occurs in one's head. One simply refuses to see oneself as less worthy than others. Thus is conceived an ideological project, according to Hewitt, whereby social subjects extend "the chain of equivalences between themselves and other subjects towards more democratic and egalitarian forms of political existence." There is, in the interviews, considerable whittling down of the reputations of the high and mighty politicians, as well as a deflation of powerful and remote service providers and moral judges. The self here is pointing outward, overcoming in imagination the dreadful constraints dealt out by reality. I wish to construe the self here as leaning towards personal agency.

When Beth expressed an interest in keeping in touch with the interviewer, she said with chagrin: "I guess your interest in me must be for the study." Note the similarity of that comment to the devastating remark the employer at the hospital made to her: "You must be here for the janitorial position." In both cases, the poor are reduced to use and function in some other schema. They are not of interest as subjects, as personal agents, but are "raw material" in other's empowerment scenarios (e.g., book). They are not chosen to be empowered, and their own personal self-empowerment is severely constrained.

So personal agency is a fundamental issue here and needs to be spelled out before presenting positive strategies of self-empowerment and change. Personal agency is more than a synonym for the action of the self; it is the self straining to engage its powers on the projects of its life. This active state is natural to optimally functioning human beings and seeks healthily to fight its way out of the obstacles that surround it. Kevin, for instance, will not quit his bad job because he would have to go on welfare while waiting to qualify for UI benefits: "I'm a very proud person. I couldn't just sit back … and go on welfare. I couldn't do that. I have to work, I have to provide for myself. I have to take care of myself. I couldn't let somebody else take care of me. It would drive me crazy. It would drive me absolutely up the wall." Crowded with "I"s, his expression conveys the strained effort of a self struggling to break free of its constraints and the grim possibilities that threaten it.

Similarly, Stephanie suggests that the self can be lost to itself but can be helped to find its way back. As a single parent, often feeling cooped up with her children, Stephanie would occasionally be provided with parent relief by her caseworker.

> Just to give me a break, so that I could get caught up in my housework, and just on myself, to do things for me. Because being

a single parent, *you lose you.* You're so busy taking care of your children and your life that you forget about you. [emphasis added]

The image here is that of a tactful state benefit causing an obstacle to be removed, having the result that the personal identity moves back into the animating center of one's action. Similarly, George's travel allowance made his training a viable reality for him and put back on the family table the food that his former travel expenses had removed. There was, again, the sense of a weight lifted and an interior energy thereby released. "The motivation was within, but it gave me the push I needed, in the right direction."

The "agency restriction" model at work here needs to confront the new deficit-cutting government responses to the alleged immobility of the poor. The government wants to tie benefits for the poor to active pursuits of training or employment. The assumption is that the poor are passive and need to be made useful by programs and training. But the poor, according to this and other studies, would be more accurately portrayed as active, but circumscribed, in their human agency. They need daycare, transportation and parent relief just to clear away the strings of contingency that entrap them. This would enable them to then take advantage of courses and opportunities. Do not cut their benefits and put the money into training if that leaves them even more hamstrung than before and enroled in courses that lead nowhere.

Wanting to Work

The vehicles of choice for leaving the cycle of reproductive practices and entering into the ownership of one's narrative are work and education. Meaningful work is like the Holy Grail to many informants. They yearned for it, for the fulfillment of both individualistic and social purposes.

Though Stephanie is planning further education on Mother's Allowance, her whole being seems pointed towards the workforce, like an arrow in a bow. She finds work to be the proper garden for the growing of the adult self. "I want to be out there working. You grow, you grow, when you're out working ... You become physically and mentally stronger. You're meeting people all the time, and you have the sense of getting more and more and more." By contrast, she finds home a regressive, diseducating place: "When you sit at home, your brain becomes mush." She goes on, seeming to envision her true self in its proper domain.

> When I get out into the working force, I feel classy, I feel that I'm doing this on my own, I'm supporting myself. I'm not getting handouts — nobody has to call me a beggar. Because I'm putting my time in, I feel that I need to put my time in to get what I'm getting. I don't feel that I'm putting my time in for my Mother's Allowance.

"Putting my time in" means that the self-reliant self is a robust net contributor to her society, not an enclaved recipient of its largesse.

While Stephanie's purpose is to engage her individual powers, John, a young member of the working poor, has a more collective orientation. He is a would-be writer and is resigned to his poverty until he finds out if he is any good. He has a part-time job helping a man repair his rental properties. When asked what he got out of his present job, he answered:

> The feeling that I am part of the community, knowing that I am helping someone accomplish his goals, maintenance and upkeep of rental dwellings. It feels good to help out, besides the money. If I'm not doing that, I'm feeling somewhat alienated.

He is not simply "putting his time in" like Stephanie; when he works he is entering into the collective story of his own community.

Education

Education was seen as a path to meaningful work and away from the minimum wage. Those who are on longer-term benefits — thus relieved from the need to find employment — were more likely to look to further schooling as the vehicle for personal improvement. Stephanie came to a turning point while at a parent support group:

> I got burned out from going and listening to all these people who are crying because they can't get out there and do things for themselves because of the system. And that's when I just got gung ho and said, "Well, *I'm* going to university." I cannot go out and get a job and go out and support my three children, being out of school for eleven years. I need to have an education to have anything more than minimum wage.

Similarly, Nancy has quit her babysitting job and all other low-wage employment to concentrate on her education. She is now upgrading, hoping to take a two-year diploma course in Library Technology. "Once I get that, then work becomes more important." She divides her time among three activities: extensive volunteer work in a school library, studying, and raising her two children.

One informant, the disabled student Mark, shaped his educational plan in a socially conscious direction. He is working towards a degree in sociology and social work, so that "I should be able hopefully to 'up' my standard of living, and I'd also like to tie my degree into dealing with social change ... so that I can help the battle." All of these rational, purposeful strategies have a payoff in the present as well as (hopefully) in the future. They reduce the stigma of receiving benefits. Most importantly, they formulate a narrative for the self to see itself as rising out of poverty. This requires more explicit attention.

Making Their Own Narrative

Nancy's view is that there are two choices for someone on Mother's Allowance: you either fester in such a system or you plan your education. In this way, you can prepare yourself for a well-paying job that will spring you from the stagnant self-interest of being "on the system." The shaping of narratives out of the grayness and stasis of poverty is a common pursuit of the informants. Sometimes these stories are actual plans, but more often than not they are prefigurings of futures hoped for. Poverty is so miserable that people in it often see themselves as in transition *out of it.* For some the consummation of this unfulfilled state is only capable of expression as a dream.

In our society where not only the means of production but also the means of welfare are no longer in people's hands, there is little or nothing that feels like one's own. So Sandra and Daniel fantasize about breaking out of the dependencies into which poverty has cast them. They dream of a rural self-sufficiency where they can make a home where the self can be at the centre of life, not on its gritty margin. When they were asked where they would like to be, they break out into a veritable duet of yearning:

SANDRA: In my own house in the country.

DANIEL: Yes, that's what both of us want.

SANDRA: A garden, chickens, they're my eggs and my meat. Maybe a cow or two for milk and beef. Pig possibly for pork. Make my own bread, and my own peace and quiet, and my own peace of mind.

DANIEL: That's the days, that's the days, you know.

SANDRA: I lived on a farm, I raised all my kids on a farm.

DANIEL: I never lived on a farm, but I've stayed on farms. And that's the way I want to live. If I could have it my way ... I would live like the Mennonites. No power, no nothing ...

SANDRA: The old saying, go back to the good old days.

DANIEL: The horse and buggy days, the best ... They're strong, the Mennonites that I've met, they're big people.

SANDRA: They're healthy.

The world they long for is not just an idealized rural past. Like Ann, they want something of their own: a house in the country, the self-provisioning of farm life. In another place they indicate they want a community that embodies mutual aid among neighbours who, presumably, will be culturally and racially like themselves. The vision, despite all its positive content, seems to have nativist roots. Their place in the country would be at the centre of a knowable world that would be fixed in time, always their own. The vision sketches a retreat (understandable in a way) from an urban maelstrom of dirt, ethnic difference, police, vomit and the feeling of being trapped. Their utopia is meant to fill the hungers of the dystopia they are living.

Building Social Connections

People invested time and energy in relationships, from the personal to the community level. Dan and Sandra are fervent on the power of love and giving to sustain oneselves in hard times. Poverty having removed all security and diminished all choice, one can still have a partner to rely on and can still choose to be loving and faithful. In Sandra's words, "Well, there is one thing what should keep people going and that's love. Without love, you're lost. You love your partner enough, you're going to work things out." Love is wise, so respects and trusts the other's need for personal space and time. When the partner goes out, she adds, "you know he's going to come back and he's not going to do anything they shouldn't be doing. You understand why they've got to get out. They have to have time to themself, they have to have time to think, they have to have their own peace, a lot of things."

Lower-income people are often creative and proactive in cultivating mutual aid networks among family and friends. With care, one can construct a familiar community of "welfare" — in the positive and non-controlling sense — where subtle reciprocities and skills exchanges allow people to give without diminishing the recipient. Thus everyday relationships outside the SSA field and marketplace can provide occasions for practices guided by community values and justice. Family members must be educated about the situation of poverty, and their forms of help should be constructive and non-stigmatizing. They should be ready to *receive* the reciprocating contribution of the low-income member as well. To construct a mutual aid network in a self-regarding, individualistic era requires organization. Being one of the working poor means that you have no state or company benefits for, say, the dental work needed by your family. If you want dental work for yourself or your children, you must cobble together your own welfare network. As Monique said: "If they're lucky they've got a good support group with their families and then their parents are paying for it. That's the only way to do it." Others borrow from their friends or, in some cases, single mothers may enlist the support of boyfriends that may or may not live in for their support of her household. To play this active role in constructing the well-being of your own family requires a root sense of entitlement to the means of livelihood and the confidence to convince others. One also has to face bureaucratic resistance to crafting one's network of support, for state rules construct its recipients in a fairly narrow familial groove.

Networks beyond family and friends are more difficult. There are of course ready-made activities and associations in public housing. George and his family have become involved in the tenants' association in their new home in London, and he is pleased so far. In contrast, Brenda does not care to use community resources geared to low-income people specifically — because she wants to avoid being stigmatized. But other informants are much more proactive in their community involvements. Julia, for instance, has tried to organize social events for the tenants of her seniors' building, but people were too fearful of their new ex-psychiatric neighbours to participate. Mark's involvement has been more successful. He does volunteer work in a coffee house which functions as a drop-in centre for ex-psychiatric patients. He helps provide them with clothing and company. Given their "own sense of individuality," Mark commented, "you have to be very careful not to make it seem like you're giving a handout." He respects the human qualities and skills of these street people: "there is a very strong core of dignity, pride and power ... They have so much to offer." Suffering from poverty himself, his constructive empathy allows him to see the street people without the configuring lenses of the service providers.

"Owning" Social Benefits

I have come to define those practices where recipients renounce their benefits or sacrifice them out of a feeling of being disentitled as "reproductive" of the social relations of poverty. Conversely, feeling and acting out of a sense of entitlement to benefits is positive and proactive. The instance we will examine is single mothers sacrificing their own nutritional needs for their children's because they felt disentitled.

Mothers such as Nancy and Stephanie sacrifice their own eating for their children's. That is a powerful maternal instinct and has positive features, but it reproduces the impoverishment of one's personal agency. The notion that children must eat well and mother's food is an afterthought harnesses a self-sacrificing motive to a socially disentitling end. After speaking of her children's food, Nancy says, "They're healthy, so that must mean something." Here she must eat a misplaced self-esteem rather than nutrition. When she gets tomato juice, "that's mine"; otherwise, she cannot compete for food that her children might eat, cannot take that food from their mouths. This self-sacrifice is a social construction crafted out of the lowered self-esteem of the poor person, but also out of the perceived non-ownership of social wages in a capitalist society. The money from Mother's Allowance is not felt to belong to the recipient, who feels guilty about taking it and only spends it in particular ways. To recall Stephanie's words: "The money that I get that comes in goes into my house and my children — I don't take it for myself." So the non-ownership of social wages comes out of capitalism but needs to be reproduced in the social psychological reactions of the poor person. To feel and act disentitled, then, was to reproduce the marginality of poverty — a recourse many other respondents resolutely rejected.

Contrary to the sacrificial and non-entitled attitude, other informants feel that when there is a need for food or other necessities,
you should take what is offered. Peter does not like being on
welfare, but he feels that you have to take welfare until you get a
job, and even then you need it for a month or so until you get paid.
"For example, if I can get into the security guard place it's going to
be a month or two until I can get off welfare, because they take off
the money for your uniform and your licence ... which is sort of
expensive." Welfare enables Peter to manage transitions in his life
in the marginal work world. A non-stigmatizing way to look at his
social assistance benefits is to see them as non-market income being
cycled into people's hands by the state as compensation for the
political economy's fragmentation of standard work. It is possible
to see these benefits without the profound moralistic baggage
attached to them — and it is progressive to do so. Similarly, Albert
insists that people on benefits stand up and insist on their rights to
societal help. This brings us to the subject of resistant practices.

Resistant and Transformative Practices

Those practices and positions which focus on fighting for rights,
personal and/or collective, could be called transformational. They
delegitimate poverty, calling it a violation of people's rights, and
oppose it in the wider, macrosocial ground that generates and
maintains poverty — welfare bureaucracies, legislatures, companies, the press and public opinion. Much resistance, however,
simply takes the form of dissent against government practices. As
Colin Gordon writes in the Foucauldian vein: "the history of
government as the 'conduct of conduct' is interwoven with the
history of dissenting 'counter-conducts'."[149]

What hand did the informants have in this? As an instance, Mark
was convinced that the poor should have the benefits of living as
their right, not just because they are perceived as a good person
by some agency. He wants to narrow the discretionary powers of
officials. He supplied a telling example. During a bus strike that
suspended his Paratransit ride, his counsellor advised him to put

---

[149] Gordon, "Governmental rationality," 5.

up a sign and hitch, just like any other student. Being disabled, this was most inconvenient; it threw him into dependence on the generosity of others. He had to thank them, be obliged to them, and hence was made to feel as though he was on a lower level than them. His vocal dissent was expressed to his worker.

Some informants had to fight for entitlements. The most assertive was Albert, a single parent. Having a child with a learning disability, he was convinced that his family would be better off if the state supported him to stay home, rather than pressure him to work. After much media scrutiny and political meetings, he and some others were instrumental in having state officials extend Family Benefits to fathers. Thus empowered, he has a strong message for others in poverty. "I think a lot of people feel powerless, sometimes I do. But you've got to stand up and speak for yourself, you can't let people walk all over you. And they will — if you let them. Social workers will ignore you if you don't make yourself heard." Albert has little patience with passive recipients of family benefits. He listens to their complaints — "Well they don't give me this and they don't give me that" — and then asks them when was the last time they saw their worker. The answer is usually that she called her worker and has not received a return call. He urges them to go directly to their worker. "You can do something. And if you don't make yourself heard, they're not going to listen. And if they don't listen, you're not going to get anywhere." If you do not bother your worker, you remain a file in someone's office.

Fighting for personal rights is a way to fight stigma and the low self-esteem of being a passive recipient — but it is taxing and high-risk. Stephanie, for example, fought her housing co-operative's decision to cut her housing subsidy because of her student loan — which they treated as extra income. She went to her Member of Parliament's office, to federal housing officials in London and Ottawa, only to be told (with a threatened eviction weeks away) that "maybe with a lot of other people kicking and screaming, they would hear it in Parliament, maybe not!" It left her embittered and disillusioned.

Fighting for rights for poor people in the community and on the national, legislative level — though not a common preoccupation of the informants — did engage a number of them in thought and action. Mark thought that the March on Poverty that groups from some southwestern Ontario cities organized did a good deal for public awareness. Organizations for single mothers, the London Union of Unemployed Workers, and other groups composed of persons who had experienced poverty, he thought, did empower their members. Dan and Sandra were laudatory about a dynamic minister in their area who worked for community interests and awareness and, in particular, the formation of non-profit housing co-ops. "Without [her] we'd be lost and so would other people ... The community needs her and a lot more like her ... She fights for our rights. If there's any problem, go see her, you know." Negative views were also expressed about advocacy for the poor. John found such groups to be biased and lacking in respect for authority. "They should not just try to stir up the poor and get them all angry at the government, when the government, I believe, is doing what the people want."

The last word will go to Stephanie, who expressed the frustration of anti-poverty politics for many low-income recipients:

> How many times have [the poverty commissioners] come out, to listen to people, to sit there and get everybody riled up — and nothing's been done? And you go to these things, and you sit there, and you do your march for peace ... and go to Toronto and fight for poverty. How the hell do these people get the money to take the bus to go to Toronto, or to take the time out? You do, you take the time out and you yell and scream and you get so frustrated, because what's that going to do? Nothing ... So there's a lot of powerlessness. I think maybe that's why a lot of us want to fight ... to get a job, to get up there into a position where maybe we can be heard.

A Concluding Word

What conclusions can we draw from this critical-interpretive study of human agency thwarted by poverty? First, we are struck by—and recognize the common humanity and normal human strivings in—the expressions of the low-income interviewees. As shown also by attitude surveys, poor people are not different from the majority in their culture or attitudes—in, say, their interest in education or children. They do not form a distinct grouping ("*the* poor") but, rather, they suffer the worst effects of a larger pattern.[150]

---

[150] R.W. Connell, "Poverty and education," 130-31.

The larger pattern is social or class inequality, and it is this pattern that must be changed.

A second conclusion is that helping the poor, or having empathy for the poor, is not enough. We need an enlarged view which allows low-income people and their standpoint to enter our lives with their own presence and voice. This is more than empathy, or feeling with others. In Benhabib's crucial point: "[V]ery empathetic individuals may be … lacking an 'enlarged mentality,' for their empathetic nature may make it difficult for them to draw the boundaries between self and other such that the standpoint of the 'concrete other' can emerge."[151] How does the other manifest herself? By processes of self-definition, engagement, dialogue, sometimes confrontation, in our presence and in our institutions. Without these encounters, we tend to construct the other by fantasy or projection (as we have seen in this study). No amount of empathy can substitute for "principles, institutions and procedures to enable articulation of the voice of 'others'."[152]

Thirdly, when we listen to low-income people, we find that they want societal opportunities, not handouts. They tell us that they need infrastructural supports, such as transportation and child care, for their own active energies to be engaged. They want an end to disincentives to work when they are on social benefits. They want decent standard jobs with security and the "occupational welfare" that accompanies a good job. They want to be recognized as mainstream Canadians and not segregated or stigmatized.

Finally, it is not enough to find ever more ingenious ways to alleviate misery, while ignoring the societal sources of this misery. Addressing the problem of poverty brings us up against a vaster objective: namely, how it is possible to develop as an individual citizen when market forces are reducing citizens to winners and losers. Moreover, if the elites can deal with the fiscal crisis at the expense of our poorest citizens, then the social rights of all citizens are no longer assured. To engage in political struggle to defend the bond of covenant between rich and poor in our country is to fight for the possibility of a humane future for generations to come.

----

[151] Seyla Benhabib, "The Generalized and the Concrete Other," 168.

[152] Ibid.

Service Providers

(N=18) All have fictitious names.

Harold

An official at the London City Food Bank, Harold is a fundamentalist Christian whose mission is to help the poor. He has led drives to have people from all walks of life contribute food, especially food companies and other corporations. He is responsible for increasing the information required of the recipients before they get their bags of food and wants to coordinate comparable food outlets to monitor claimants of "free" food so that they do not exploit the system. A figure of the Christian right, he wants a social community of business people, helpers like himself, and the wounded poor in need of healing. Government intervention and welfare rights are anathema to him, since they coddle the poor and do not help them overcome their problems.

Kenneth

Kenneth is a director of the long-standing Christian Army's social services for men. The organization runs rehabilitation and addiction drop-in centres, thrift stores, and hostels to house low-income men, some local, others transient. For the residential services, city welfare pays a per diem rate amount, which amounts to about half of the total funding, with the other half coming from fund-raising campaigns and the revenue from the stores. They use about 40 paid staff and a small number of volunteers. Kenneth is in accord with the organization's traditional emphasis on giving the men soup and salvation, food for the body and the soul. But he regrets that the poor have too many outlets for food and can work the system and that they will not submit to his religious or practical advice and direction. He directed operations in a smaller city in the Maritimes and yearns for the coordination and monitoring that the various helping agencies and churches achieved there.

Monique

She works in an emergency shelter for women and families. The house, with locked doors and a controlled entry, has a single women's residence at one end and a families' residence at the other. The people at this shelter are women and families who are temporarily homeless, whether due to eviction, transiency, lifestyle problems, or marital abuse. The per diem from the city does not meet the actual per diem expense, so the shelter relies on donations. The space is so inadequate that families are crowded into one room, with all the attendant problems of that arrangement. When they are very busy, which is often, they help place people in other shelters and accommodations and refer them to relevant agencies. At such hectic times, Monique regrets that their counselling and referrals are simply not meeting the needs and that people flow back into their old situations without any enduring gain or support. She has very strong empathy with the situation of poor and homeless women.

Angela

Angela is a lawyer and official in Community Legal Aid (CLA), funded by the Ministry of the Attorney General to the Law Society of Upper Canada, which administers legal aid. Meant to be an unintimidating entry point for poor people to the legal system, CLA makes many referrals as well as going to court for its clients. Poverty entails problems over eligibility for social assistance, benefit levels, appeals over the cutting off of subsidies, and landlord and tenant relations. Until they became short-staffed, they used to do community education for low-income groups and law reform projects — but now they are limited to handling the rising tide of individual cases. Angela reports that members of the client group sit on the Board of Directors which keeps them in touch with the daily concerns of poor people.

Joan (Reverend)

She is a minister with one of the Protestant denominations, whose ministry is with the urban poor in a section of London. Her task is to identify needs of the poor there and inform both the Church and social services of her findings so that those needs could be better met. In the process of fulfilling these tasks of her ministry, she has become a prominent leader and advocate for poor people. Among her activities has been an effort to convert a troubled zone of public housing to a non-profit housing co-operative, but the funding for this project has succumbed to the Conservative government chopping block in 1995. A formative experience for Joan was a course in urban social relations which required her to be a street person without money for three days. The analysis of the social structure that the course stimulated has developed into a systematic critique of the economic system which victimizes poor people and the social service/charity models which accommodate to poverty.

Duncan

Duncan is a director of a Catholic, parish-based, charity organization which responds to requests for help by disadvantaged families. Two organization people go to the low-income person's home, conduct a fairly intensive interview about background, needs, and means, and perform a brief home inspection. Sometimes he sees beer in the home, which he sees as a mark of their dissoluteness and need for escape. His workers are more likely to be called when the welfare cheque runs out within ten or so days before the end of the month. They may be asked to pay a hydro bill or supply food or gas. Before Duncan came, the organization gave cash to people, but he switched to vouchers to control consumption and avoid abuse. He thinks that 90 percent of the poor simply want to exist on handouts, so he opposes food banks which gives bags of food to the poor instead of what they really need — counselling and personal contact.

Joseph

Joseph is a director of the London Anti-Poverty organization which was started by him and other laid-off workers from the early 1980s recession. Their organization has done advocacy work on behalf of individuals who have suffered at the hand of landlords or bureaucrats. But efforts in recent years have been in organizing group protests. An example is helping single mothers fight against the local utility shutting off electricity in poor homes. The analysis of poverty is radical, seeing its roots in the growing inequality of capitalist society. So is the practice, which is directed towards alliance-making with social justice groups and unions and forming collective protests against those elites at the political or corporate level who are keeping the poor in their subordinate place.

Laureen (Sister)

Laureen is an official of a "hospitality centre" or soup kitchen in the east end which is run by a religious order of sisters. Among those who come in for a meal are ex-psychiatric patients, welfare recipients, pensioners, and those on disability. The centre provides fruits, vegetables, meats, grains, and so forth. She aims to provide a non-judgmental service with an informal and friendly community feel. It is not always easy to find volunteers who want to do the cooking and who also feel comfortable with and accept low-income people. She hopes to create a place for the poor to come to that is theirs and not anybody else's. Her impression is that some of the people are frustrated that they cannot get out of poverty, and others are more even-tempered because they have given up and feel they will never make it.

Suzette

She is a Client Services officer at Employment & Immigration Canada, giving information to Unemployment Insurance recipients with special concerns or difficulties (e.g., language problems). Her answers were comfortably specific when the questions involved UI, but elusive and hesitant when the questions turned to overall poverty issues. She indicated that she had private opinions which would be alright to discuss over coffee, but she could not comment on wider issues or critiques of UI during the interview. Suzette seemed pleased with the ministry's recent emphasis on training, which was announced along with the Conservative party cuts to the program.

Joanne

She is an official with the Abused Women's Advocacy Clinic which counsels and supports women who are suffering violence in their close relationships. It serves as advocate for client in the justice, medical, and social service field. It makes referrals to other services and conducts educational workshops through out the city. Joanne is critical of London's obliviousness to the poverty in its midst. She thinks that the city real estate market has priced the poor out of affordable housing. The charity model is often humiliating for the recipient, and she favours a coordination of social services geared to an empowerment of low-income persons.

Chris

Chris is a government worker on the London Access to Housing Committee. The Committee runs an activity centre to provide sociability for people who may be isolated in their own homes. Referrals are made for people who have psychiatric disabilities. Chris does research and advocacy on how to secure permanent housing for disadvantaged groups such as ex-psychiatric patients, immigrants, single mothers, and so on. He also looks into neighbourhoods that may be amenable to transition houses, shelters, and half-way houses. He is very aware of the obstacles to the poor being integrated into good urban neighbourhoods — the inherent biases of the commercial approach to real estate, discrimination by communities and landlords, and the complicity of urban politicians with the dominant players in the current housing scene.

Sheila

She is with Women Immigrant Services which offer individual and group counselling to assist the integration of immigrant women into Canadian society. They offer work force preparation such as skills identification, English instruction, and technical training in office work, customer and food service. The weak English language skills of women immigrants, according to Sheila, often make Canadians think that these women are stupid or slow. Job discrimination and their pressing need for funds force such women into jobs below their qualifications and puts them into housing arrangements where large families live in one-bedroom apartments.

Patricia

Street Aid Christian Mission, where Patricia works, is for disadvantaged persons. Although firstly a drop-in centre, it also offers advocacy; marriage, financial and religious counselling; clothing vouchers useable at missions and thrift stores; life skills; continuing education; Christian services; and recreational activities. Often Street Aid handles ex-psychiatric patients who Patricia feels should not have been released from psychiatric facilities in hospitals. Her husband, an ex-motorcyclist with a rough past, had had a born-again experience and decided to open a mission for street kids who did not trust social agencies as a place to stay until they got on their feet. A very hard worker, Patricia often dealt with volatile situations of young people, and tried to cope without bringing in the police. She has had a vast experience of dealing with street people and their problems.

Colleen (Reverend)

Colleen has been a chaplain at a public housing area in north London. She was asked to be a Christian presence in the community. She is a good listener with good rapport and has built up trust through polite, low-key visits to people in the community. There are 160 townhouses, most of which accommodate families led by sole support mothers. While the housing quality is adequate, the housing authority has a slow bureaucratic response to requests for repairs. All around them are fine single family homes and, on one side, the very rich. The main problem with the complex is the sense of being isolated, stigmatized, and discriminated against. It feels like apartheid, the way they are boxed in and separated from the life of the non-poor. Feeling close to the struggling people in the units, Colleen tries to build up mutual aid and community.

Donald (Father)

A priest-academic by profession and calling, Donald has devoted much of his life to speaking about, and working for, the disadvantaged. While involved with parish work, he had a great deal of personal contact with the poor. But as a teacher of men in the seminary, his pursuits have been a mixture of teaching and writing about social issues and working on committees and boards having to do with co-operative housing and other ventures aimed at improving the life of low-income people. Donald has worked out an analysis of poverty that criticizes the market economy, the tax system (which favours the rich), and the obsession of the government with the debt and the deficit while neglecting the needs of people for jobs. He believes that everyone has a right to a decent life with no stigma attached and wants to work for those structures of justice that will achieve those goals.

Jacob

Jacob is a senior official at a mission for men, aimed at the rehabilitation and accommodation of homeless, destitute, and transient men. They also provide emergency food, counselling, and referrals.

Men, including the mentally disabled, are helped to manage budgets, handle medication, and develop lifeskills. Coming up from footloose poverty himself, Jacob has learned much about himself and being poor. His experience is offered to the men as a basis of rapport and validation, while hopefully serving as a model for the struggle out of the depths of poverty. Gentle and unobtrusive, he is attentive to needs and does not moralize heavily with the men.

Doris

Working out of offices in the police station, Doris is a worker with the Family Mediation Service. When the police are called to deal with family disputes, she and perhaps one of the other workers go into the house and attempt to cool down the combatants. Each partner is talked to separately, to piece together an account of what has happened. Then there is an assessment of how the tension can be defused in the short-term and how the deeper problems can be addressed in the longer-term (e.g., mediation talk, counselling session later, referral). So great is the diversity of the problems they face (elder abuse, victim services, family violence, multicultural complexities) that their small number of workers risk staff burnout. There are ambiguities in their police alliance as well — they are seen as a "soft" service, thus more vulnerable to cuts. Also, they cannot really advocate on behalf of the client against the police.

Margaret

She is the director of the city welfare department. Very modern and professional in demeanour, she distanced herself from the excesses of the older welfare system ("the man in the house" rule). As well, she made comments designated as personal (and unattributable) to allow her a wider-ranging discourse than her official position would permit. Margaret knows that the bureaucracy is unwieldy and unresponsive at times, and its forms are sometimes so complex that even the worker struggles with them. She does not feel that the people who call her office about the poor who drink beer, for example, have any business intruding on personal tastes of fellow citizens. For all this, she still maintained a commitment to the system imperatives.

Low-Income Informants

(N=19) All have fictitious names.

Michele

Michele is a single mother in her thirties living with her 4-year-old son and grandfather (living there until he finds a place to live) in a rather shoddy unit in an otherwise good complex of subsidized housing. She is on Mother's Allowance ($649 a month) to help her with her son but is determined to get off as soon as she can. Food money fluctuates from $100 to $200 a month. She uses the food bank and Christian Soldiers organization. Transportation is hard for her to afford; she'd like a bus pass.

Robert

A single pensioner in his late sixties living on Veterans Benefits, Old Age Security, Canada Pension and GAINS—giving him about $800 a month, Robert uses the food bank and the soup kitchen and receives a food basket every three months from a downtown church. He lives in the east end, which is his stomping grounds, near the thrift store and the people and shopping he likes. A one-time alcoholic, he is mostly sober and content with his lifestyle.

John

This young man has been poor for about six years, working a lot of minimum wage jobs. He is critical of many marginal jobs — of the low wages, of their poor working conditions, and of the way the employers treat their workers. He wants to be independent. John accepts his poverty as transitional, while he establishes himself, preferably, as a writer or a journalist.

Louise

She is 58, living in a clean bright apartment over a barber shop on a $500-a-month disability pension — for which she waited for two anxious years. She is not in good health. She feels stuck, having been divorced from her husband four years ago and missing the easy travelling and proximity of friends in her native Holland. Though involved in her church, the lack of affordable transportation makes her feel isolated, and it does not help that she is not allowed to earn outside money (cleaning houses, which was her former work). Because her income is frozen, she feels she must move from her apartment to a subsidized seniors high-rise apartment. Her son and his wife live in a basement apartment in the same building.

Ann

Ann, who is 77, makes $582 a month from Old Age Security (OAS) and Canada Pension. She lives in her own home, bought three years ago. Having a Grade 6 education, she worked from age 10 to 70 at minimum wage jobs, which never allowed her to save money. With a mortgage of $745 a month, plus house insurance, heat, utilities, food, and transportation, she needs another $500 to get by. Her sons have helped her up to now but are less able to keep up regular help. She has a fierce attachment to her house and is emotional about her poverty.

Nancy

Nancy is a single mother of 41 years with two children (ages 10 and 12), who is on Mother's Allowance and lives in subsidized housing. She has a university degree. Her monthly income is $860 a month, encompassing Family Benefits and Baby Bonus. She sacrifices for her children, especially when it comes to food. She is not looking for work right now because the available work is marginal and low-paid. She is concentrating on her education and volunteer work, readying herself to take a two-year diploma course in library technology. She loves books and wants to be a library technician.

Beth

Beth is a single woman in her forties who has struggled with poverty all her life. Family unrest and poverty forced her to quit school at Grade 9. Since she was 20, she has been slowly upgrading her education. Her dream is to become a scientist. She has health problems, which means strong (expensive) medications that have affected her energy level and memory. Finally getting her degree, she accumulated extensive OSAP (Ontario Student Assistance Program) debts. During that time, she lived with her mother who is ill and became dependent on Beth's housework and general support. She cannot afford to move out, so is very stressed out with home responsibilities, lack of money, and a part-time marginal job that even hampers her ability to find additional work. She was embittered by an early experience with welfare, so doesn't want to resort to it.

Mark

Mark is a 35-year-old single man who is physically disabled. He is attending King's College at the University of Western Ontario studying social work and sociology, while living with his parents (to whom he pays $250 a month for room and board). He gets $561 a month in disability benefits under Family Benefits. Mark has a strong sense of his rights and entitlements and has fought for his interests at the college. He is involved as a volunteer in the London Coffee House, a social organization providing a drop-in facility for ex-psychiatric patients.

Peter

A young man of 22, he is a member of the working poor. He has been struggling to attain stable employment in the last few years, but to no avail. He has been laid off, bored with work, harassed by his boss and disillusioned with the working conditions of his various job stints. His damp and musty basement apartment is poorly serviced by what he considers his "slum landlord." Peter is making $413 on general welfare and would much rather work. With his present educational level of Grade 12, he finds himself stuck in minimum wage jobs. He has been training as a cook with the London Youth Project but found the experience unhelpful.

Julia

A proud, gentle 70-year old, she wanted to be interviewed to express her concern about the forced choices imposed on one by subsidized housing. She moved from Toronto to London to be with her husband who was having an operation at the hospital. When he eventually died, her reduced financial circumstances put her into subsidized housing in London, although she really wanted to go back to Toronto. Furthermore, she is unhappy at the decision to turn her building from a seniors' building into an adult building with ex-psychiatric patients. This has forced the seniors to stay in their apartments because of their fear of these ex-patients.

Stephanie

Stephanie is a single mother with three girls (who had been abused by their father) who fled Ottawa for London where they have lived for two years. Her children are just starting school. She is on Mother's Allowance, relying on some support from her father ($50 a month or so). She begged and lobbied to get into co-operative housing where her housing charge is geared to income. Stephanie started university with the help of an OSAP loan, which caused the co-op to raise her housing charge — all of which she is currently fighting through Neighbourhood Legal Services. At the same time, she fought to get daycare from the city while she took her three university courses (they insisted that she needed to be enrolled in 3 1/2 courses). This led to a nervous breakdown and her children needed to be put up with social services.

Kate

A single mother on Mother's Allowance, Kate returned to school and received a B.A. with top marks. She is sharing a house with her sister and has a comfortable lifestyle. One frustration is that social work schools are rejecting her application, keeping her from an occupational dream of hers. She feels the second-rate status of being a single parent on Mother's Allowance and has lost touch with her married-couple friends.

Brenda

A single mother on Mother's Allowance, she lives with her two teenage sons in an apartment. She had lived in a low-rental basement apartment in a part of town that she was ashamed of. When she regained custody of her kids after overcoming a bout of alcoholism, she decided to move into a bright, clean apartment with hardwood floors — but it cost her $300 more than the other place. That means that the food situation isn't very good. She's delighted to live in a kind of place that she used to do cleaning in, but it's somewhat small and her neighbours are noisy, so she may move. She feels somewhat isolated. She works "under the table" cleaning people's houses on a part-time basis. She wants to go back to school to finish her education. Having been poor all her life, she is determined to rise out of poverty.

Judith

She lives with her children in a normal rental unit. Since being on Mother's Allowance for the last year, she feels looked down upon, by bank tellers and social workers. She is against ghettoizing economic groups.

Albert

A disabled single father living in an unsubsidized apartment with a son, 16, and a daughter, 14, Albert is on Family Benefits — which he was instrumental in getting extended to male parents. While he used to drive a truck, he has been a full-time dad for almost 14 years, of which ten have been on benefits. Combining Father's Allowance and Disability ($170 a month), he receives $1262 a month, but must spend $575 on rent, then heat and hydro, bus passes, phone, and food. Money ends up being quite tight — but he's getting better benefits for himself and his children than he used to get driving a truck at minimum wage. He used to drink heavily, but that is in the past. His eye problems make challenging work difficult to obtain, but he has a dream of getting into computers.

Daniel and Sandra

Daniel and his wife, Sandra, act as superintendent of a subsidized townhouse complex which is occupied by many recent immigrants and refugees and having its share of social problems. Their compensation is free rent. They have come to resent the Cambodians who are the most recent arrivals and don't understand their customs. Their nerves are jangled by the tumult and filth of the place, and they yearn for the country. Sandra is on disability, which limits Daniel's qualification for benefits, so he is forced to work at marginal minimum wage jobs. They are just getting by materially and are very bitter that Daniel was denied UI because he told the truth about his helping with the buildings.

Kevin

Kevin is living in a housing co-op. After being laid off from Algoma Steel in Sault St. Marie in the early 1980s, he could only get poor jobs, so experienced real poverty. His marriage broke up, leaving him with little furniture or material means. He has worked in a photographic chain store, working in very unsafe conditions for low pay. Poverty makes him look shabby and he has difficulty in meeting women.

George

Married with two children, George lives in subsidized housing. He is taking courses in Child and Youth Work at a community college. He feels a little displaced as his network is in a nearby city, St. Thomas. But he felt he had to move to be near the community college to take advantage of the larger number of jobs he hopes to qualify for when he's done. He is from a family in New Brunswick where he was laid off and jobless for two years. After such hardship, he moved to Ontario and picked tomatoes and tobacco, and was finally able to bring his family as well. He had difficulty finding auto body work, for which he had apprenticed in the Maritimes until the bottom fell out of the industry. His health deteriorated, and he hinted at head damage and mental disturbance. He is struggling with academics. His wife can't work as long as he is in school and on benefits.

Rebecca

[An "almost-interview"] Rebecca called in tears to put off her appointment because she needed to pick up her child at camp because he was suicidal: "He has had a rough life." Having been just beaten up by a man this weekend, she was in no shape to have her son home, so she was putting him in a shelter called Merrymount.

References

Ad Hoc Collective of London, Ontario, "Some cuts don't heal" (pamphlet), Fall 1995.

Benhabib, Seyla. "The Generalized and the Concrete Other: The Kohlberg-Gilligan Controversy." In S. Benhabib, *Situating the Self: Gender, Community and Postmodernism in Contemporary Ethics*. New York: Routledge, 1992, 148–177.

Bourdieu, Pierre. *Invitation to a Reflexive Sociology*. Chicago: University of Chicago Press, 1992.

Bowles, Samuel and Herbert Gintis, *Democracy and Capitalism*. New York: Basic Books, 1986.

Bulmer, Martin, Jane Lewis, and David Piachaud, eds., *Goals of Social Policy*. London: Unwin Hyman, 1989.

Canada, *Health Insurance*, Report of the Advisory Committee on Health Insurance. Ottawa: Minister of Pensions and National Health, 1943 (the "Heagerty report").

Canada, Parliament, House of Commons, Advisory Committee on Reconstruction, *Housing and Community Planning, Final Report of the Sub-committee*, March 24, 1944. Ottawa: 1946, 339 (the "Curtis report").

Canada, *Report on Social Security for Canada*. Prepared for the Advisory Committee on Reconstruction, House of Commons, Special Committee on Social Security (the "Marsh report"). Ottawa, 1943.

Clarke, John. "Ontario's social movements — the struggle intensifies." In Colin Leys and Marguerits Mendell, eds., *Culture and Social Change: Social Movements in Québec and Ontario*. Montréal: Black Rose Books, 1992, 213–224.

Connell, R.W. "Poverty and education," *Harvard Educaitonal Review* 64:2 (Summer 1994), 125-49.

Connell, R. W. "States, powers and genders," World Congress of Sociology, Bielefeld, Germany, (July 19, 1994).

Culpitt, Ian. *Welfare and Citizenship: Beyond the Crisis of the Welfare State*. London: Sage, 1992.

Dean, Mitchell. "'A social structure of many souls': Moral regulation, government, and self-formation," *Canadian Journal of Sociology,* 19:2 (1994), 145–168.

Donnison, David. "Social policy: the community-based approach." In Martin Bulmer, Jane Lewis and David Piachaud, eds., *The Goals of Social Policy*. London: Unwin Hyman, 1989, 199–220.

Duffy, Ann and Nancy Mandell, "The widening gap: social inequality and poverty." In Dan Glenday and Ann Duffy, eds., *Canadian Society: Understanding and Surviving in the 1990s*. Toronto: McClelland and Stewart, 1994, 49–85.

Esping-Andersen, Gosta. "Labour movements and the welfare state: alternatives in the 1990s." In Daniel Drache, ed., *Getting On Track: Social Democratic Strategies for Ontario*. Montreal: McGill-Queens University Press, 1992, 58.

----------. "The Three Political Economies of the Welfare State." *Canadian Review of Sociology and Anthropology* 26: 1 (February 1989), 10–36.

Foucault, Michel. "Nietzsche, Genealogy, History." In *The Foucault Reader*. New York: Pantheon, 1984, 76-100.

Fraser, Nancy. "Struggle over needs: outline of a socialist-feminist critical theory." In Nancy Fraser, *Unruly Practices: Power, Discourse and Gender in Contemporary Social Theory*. Cambridge, U.K.: Polity Press, 1989, 161–187.

----------. "Women, Welfare, and the Politics of Need Interpretation." In Nancy Fraser, *Unruly Practices: Power, Discourse and Gender in Contemporary Social Theory*. Cambridge, U.K.: Polity Press, 1989, 144–160.

Gordon, Colin. "Governmental Rationality: An Introduction." In Graham Burchell, Colin Gordon and Peter Miller, eds., *The Foucault Effect: Studies in Governmentality,* Chicago: University of Chicago Press, 1991, 1-51.

Guest, Dennis. *The Emergence of Social Security in Canada*. Vancouver: University of British Columbia Press, 1980.

----------. "World War II and the welfare state in Canada." In Allan Moscovitch and Jim Albert, eds., *The Benevolent State: The Growth of Welfare in Canada*. Toronto: Garamond, 1987, 205–221.

Habermas, Jurgen. "Historical materialism and the development of normative structures." In Jurgen Habermas (Ed), *Communication and the Evolution of Society*. Boston: Beacon Press, 1979, 95-129.

Harris, Ralph. *Beyond the Welfare State*. London: Institute of Economic Affairs, 1988.

Heidenheim, Paul. "The Political Economy of Canadian Public Assistance." Master's Thesis, Dept. of Sociology, University of Western Ontario, 1984.

Hewitt, Martin. *Welfare, Ideology and Need: Developing Perspectives on the Welfare State*. Hertfordshire: Harvester Wheatsheaf, 1992.

hooks, bell. *Outlaw Culture: Resisting Representations*. New York: Routledge, 1994.

Hulchanski, J. David. "Ontario's blow to residential apartheid: legalizing apartments in houses," *Perception*, 18:2 (November 1994), 25-28.

Kerans, Patrick. "Need and welfare: 'thin' and 'thick' approaches." In Andrew F. Johnson, Stephen McBride and Patrick J. Smith eds., *Continuities and Discontinuities: The Political Economy of Social Welfare* Toronto: University of Toronto Press, 1994, 44–61.

Lewis, Jane. "Chapter 6: Introduction." In Martin Bulmer, Jane Lewis and David Piachaud, eds., *The Goals of Social Policy*. London: Unwin Hyman, 1989, 131–140.

Miller, S.M., "Community development and the underclass." In Martin Blumer, Jane Lewis, and David Peachaud (Eds.), *Goals of Social Policy*. London: Unwin Hyman, 1989, 221-27.

Miller, S.M. "Poverty and respect: social identity and public policy," World Congress of Sociology, Bielefeld, Germany, July 1994.

Moscovitch, Allan and Glenn Drover, "Social expenditures and the welfare state: the Canadian experience." In Allan Moscovitch and Jim Albert, eds., *The Benevolent State: The Growth of Welfare in Canada*. Toronto: Garamond, 1987, 13–43.

Mullaly, Robert. "Social welfare and the new right: a class mobilization perspective." In Andrew Johnson, Stephen McBride and Patrick J. Smith, eds., *Continuities and Discontinuities: The Political Economy of Social Welfare*. Toronto: University of Toronto Press, 1994, 76–94.

Muszynski, Leon. "A new social welfare agenda for Canada." In Daniel Drache, ed., *Getting On Track: Social Democratic Strategies for Ontario*. Montreal: McGill-Queens University Press, 1992, 170–185.

----------. "Defending the welfare state and labour market policy." In Andrew Johnson, Stephen McBride and Patrick J. Smith, eds., *Continuities and Discontinuities: The Political Economy of Social Welfare*. Toronto: University of Toronto Press, 1994, 306–326.

National Council of Welfare. *A Blueprint for Social Security Reform*. Ottawa: Supply and Service, 1994.

Nietzsche, Friedrich. "The antichrist." In Walter Kaufmann, ed., *The Portable Nietzsche*. New York: Viking, 1968, 565–656.

Offe, Claus. *Disorganized Capitalism*. Cambridge: Polity Press, 1987.

Panitch, Leo. "Changing gears: democratizing the welfare state." In Andrew Johnson, Stephen McBride and Patrick J. Smith, eds., *Continuities and Discontinuities: The Political Economy of Social Welfare*. Toronto: University of Toronto Press, 1994, 36–43.

Procacci, Giovanna. "Social economy and the government of poverty." In Graham Burchell, Colin Gordon and Peter Miller, eds., *The Foucault Effect: Studies in Governmentality*. Chicago: University of Chicago Press, 1991, 151–168.

Reich, Dahlia. "Nutritious meals too costly for majority on welfare," *London Free Press*, March 25 (1989), C2.

Rooke, Patricia T. and R.L. Schnell. "Guttersnipes and charity children: 19th century child rescue in the Atlantic Provinces." In Patricia Rooke and R.L. Schnell, eds., *Studies in Childhood History: A Canadian Perspective*. Calgary, Alta: Detselig Enterprises, 1982, 82–104.

Ross, David P., E. Richard Shillington, and Clarence Lochhead. *The Canadian Fact Book on Poverty*. Ottawa: Canadian Council on Social Development, 1994.

Saldov, Morris. "Unemployment and Social Work: Community Initiatives for a Preventive Approach." In Graham Riches and Gordon Ternowetsky, eds., *Unemployment and Welfare: Social Policy & the Work of Social Work*. Toronto: Garamond, 1992, 213–222.

Squires, Peter. *Anti-social Policy: Welfare, Ideology and the Disciplinary State.* New York: Harvester Wheatsheaf, 1990.

Taylor-Gooby, Peter. *Social Change, Social Welfare and Social Science.* Toronto: University of Toronto Press, 1991.

Toupin, Lynne. "Index on workfare." *Canadian Forum* (October, 1995), 47-50.

Turner, Joanne C. "The Historical Base." In Joanne Turner, and Francis J. Turner, eds., *Canadian Social Welfare.* Don Mills, Ont.: Collier Macmillan Canada, 1981, 49–57.

Ursel, Jane. "The State and the Maintenance of Patriarchy: A Case Study of Family, Labour, and Welfare Legislation in Canada." In James Dickinson and Bob Russell, eds., *Family, Economy and State: The Social Reproduction Process Under Capitalism.* Toronto: Garamond, 1986, 150–191.

Wolfe, Alan. *Whose Keeper? Social Science and Moral Obligation.* Berkeley: University of California Press, 1989.

Yalnizyan, Armine. "Securing society: Creating Canadian social policy." In Armine Yalnizyan, T. Ran Ide and Arthur Cordell, eds., *Shifting Time: Social Policy and the Future of Work.* Toronto: Between the Lines, 1994, 17–71.

Name Index

Subject Index